# MY INCREDIBLE
## *Journey*

# MY INCREDIBLE
## *Journey*

ROXANN JEWETT GOODWIN

Xulon Press
2301 Lucien Way #415
Maitland, FL 32751
407.339.4217
www.xulonpress.com

© 2020 by Roxann Jewett Goodwin

Copy Editor Heather Caruso
Foreword by Steve Reynolds
Epilogue by Jana Goodwin Moritz

All rights reserved solely by the author. The author guarantees all contents are original and do not infringe upon the legal rights of any other person or work. No part of this book may be reproduced in any form without the permission of the author. The views expressed in this book are not necessarily those of the publisher.

The events and conversations in this book have been set down to the best of the author's ability, although some names and titles have been changed or omitted to protect the privacy of the individuals.

Unless otherwise indicated, Scripture quotations taken from the King James Version (KJV)–*public domain.*

Scripture quotations marked (NLT) are taken from the Holy Bible, New Living Translation, copyright © 1996, 2004, 2007, 2013, 2015 by Tyndale House Foundation. Used by permission of Tyndale House Publishers, Inc., Carol Stream, Illinois 60188. All rights reserved.

Printed in the United States of America.

ISBN-13: 978-1-63221-242-9

To the faithful persecuted believers in the Southeast Asia countries who have allowed us to come alongside you to reach your own people for His kingdom. God knows who you are, and we have been blessed and honored to work beside you.

# Table of Contents

*Foreword by Steve Reynolds* . . . . . . . . . . . . . . . . . . . . . . . . . . . . ix
*Acknowledgments* . . . . . . . . . . . . . . . . . . . . . . . . . . . . . . . . . . . . xi

Chapter 1: A Little Girl's Story . . . . . . . . . . . . . . . . . . . . . . . . . 1
Chapter 2: A Little Boy's Story . . . . . . . . . . . . . . . . . . . . . . . . . 9
Chapter 3: Boy Marries Girl . . . . . . . . . . . . . . . . . . . . . . . . . . . 15
Chapter 4: Provisions . . . . . . . . . . . . . . . . . . . . . . . . . . . . . . . . 25
Chapter 5: Stepping Out in Faith . . . . . . . . . . . . . . . . . . . . . . . 33
Chapter 6: Paving a New Path . . . . . . . . . . . . . . . . . . . . . . . . . 45
Chapter 7: If God is in it … . . . . . . . . . . . . . . . . . . . . . . . . . . . 53
Chapter 8: Overcoming Hurdles . . . . . . . . . . . . . . . . . . . . . . . 91
Chapter 9: God's Faithfulness to the End . . . . . . . . . . . . . . . 117
Chapter 10: A New Tomorrow . . . . . . . . . . . . . . . . . . . . . . . . 131

*Epilogue by Jana Goodwin Moritz* . . . . . . . . . . . . . . . . . . . . . 153
*About the Author* . . . . . . . . . . . . . . . . . . . . . . . . . . . . . . . . . . 155
*How to Know for Sure that You are Going to Heaven* . . . . . . . . 157

# Foreword

I first met Otis and Roxann in 1984. I was a young church planter in the Washington, D.C. metro area when I received a message that a missionary had called the church office and wanted to speak with me. My initial response was that it was just another phone call from a missionary wanting money and support. I had received many phone calls like that before, so I have to admit I was a bit cynical. But I called him back, and that was a decision I always look back on with gratitude that I did it.

That phone call started a relationship that spanned decades between both of our families. Otis was a great friend and mentor to me, and I had the joy of serving as his pastor from 1984 until his passing. I was there as his ministry was just forming, through the trials of ministry transition, at the birth of Outreach To Asia Nationals (OTAN), and throughout the incredible ministry to the people of Southeast Asia. And what a ministry it has been!

Through the work of Otis and Roxann's ministry, countless thousands of lives have been changed. The story you are about to read – their story – is not just one of two people's lives. It's a story of hardships, perseverance, endurance, courage, and ultimately joy. It's the story of two people who obediently stepped out on faith to fulfill God's call on their lives to serve in full-time global mission's ministry.

One of the hardest things I have to do in ministry is perform the funerals of people who I have loved and served with in ministry. I was there at the beginning of Otis' ministry and the birth of OTAN, and I was there at the end of his life when he went home to be with our Lord. Otis fought the good fight until the very end. His heart was willing to do more for the gospel here on earth, but his body was sick and broken and could no longer sustain him. I miss him greatly, but the work still goes on!

As you read this book, I encourage you to open your heart and mind to the possibility that God is calling you to more. Be bold and courageous and ask God this question, "What more do you want me to do for the sake of the gospel?"

Roxann's intent in writing this book is not to draw attention, fame, or glory to herself but rather to God and the wondrous works and miracles He did in their life. OTAN is an organization that is still committed to training and equipping persecuted Asian pastors. I encourage you to check out what they're currently doing in Asia. You can find more information at *www.otan.org*.

Steve Reynolds
Lead Pastor at Capital Baptist Church, Annandale, Virginia
Chairman of the Board, OTAN

# Acknowledgments

To my husband whom the Lord called home just before our 49th wedding anniversary. We started this *Incredible Journey* when we were in the eighth grade, and what a journey it has been.

To my three beautiful daughters and your husbands – Kimberly and Randy, Julie and Glen, Jana and Gary. You girls have been a blessing since you were born, and you have given us five amazing grandsons and four lovely granddaughters.

To my grandchildren – Joshua and wife Becky; Corey and wife Kara; Lee and wife Audra; Michael and wife Rebekah; Andrew and wife Chelsea; Kristina and husband Dana; Jessica, Jaden and Josalyn; as well as my 15 great-grandchildren – Ashton, Jeremiah, Phillip, William, Megan, Roxann, Emma, Joshua, Mason, Jacob, Jonah, Maria, Blake, Maggie, and Boaz Otis plus all who are yet to be born, I pray you are the next generations to carry the Lord's ministry into the world.

To our faithful prayer and financial supporters, without you we could not have gone on this journey of serving the Lord. What an amazing support system we have had all these years.

To the wonderful and faithful staff that the Lord gave us through the years and all the volunteers who have served in the ministry of OTAN and BTW. To each of you, I will ever be grateful. To our OTAN Board of Directors, thank you for your faithful support and service.

To Bill and Jan Olson for your faithful professional guidance and personal friendship and support.

To Don and Rita Powell for the many years of friendship and support beyond measure.

To Kimberly, my faithful and sweet travel companion. Thank you for your many hours producing curriculum, your ability to connect with the ladies in teaching and training, and the love you have shown to all the women who have been part of the ministry. Last but not least, the respect that you have shown me always in all the years we have traveled and served together. You are like a daughter to me.

To Lois Morey and Gary and Jana Moritz who spent many long hours proofreading this book. Thank you for your encouragement.

To Sandie Powell for your ideas and suggestions as I began this book.

To Heather Caruso for your help and assistance getting this book ready for print.

To Glen Michael Bailey for your insight into the cover design.

# 1

# A Little Girl's Story

> For since the beginning of the world men have not heard, nor perceived by the ear, neither hath the eye seen, O God, beside thee, what he hath prepared for him that waiteth for him.
>
> Isaiah 64:4 KJV

When Isaiah penned these words thousands of years ago, God knew at that time exactly how He would need to guide, lead, and carry me through blessings and challenges along my remarkable and unique, albeit at times, almost unbelievable journey. God would be the bulwark for Otis and me as well as for our marriage, our family, and our ministry.

October 29, 1939 in Gardiner, Maine, Clinton "Ted" Jewett and Doris Louise Noyes Jewett celebrated the birth of their second child, Roxann Jean. My older brother, Clinton Noyes, was 5 years old when I joined the family. In the next eight years, Gail Elizabeth and Sally Louise would be born, completing our family.

We made our home in the small rural bedroom community of Whitefield, Maine joining the previous generations of my father. All my father's family lived there, died there, and are buried there, including Otis, in the same cemetery.

My father experienced deep tragedy at the age of 13. His father, Frank Jewett, the deputy sheriff, had a man who was on probation under his authority. This responsibility led to an explosive and horrendous series of criminal events. The man went into my father's home and killed his mother and 15-year-old brother. Next, the man, obviously deranged, went home and murdered his own wife and mother-in-law and then turned the gun on himself committing suicide. A short four years later, his father died too.

In spite of this terrible tragedy experienced at such a young, impressionable age, my father went on to school and graduated from Coburn Classical Institute in Waterville, Maine. He married my mother Doris Louise Noyes from Jefferson, Maine in 1933. My father led a productive, successful life providing for my family.

My dad was a dairy farmer. My early years were filled with hard work. I learned to drive a tractor before I learned to drive a car. I worked alongside the farmhands during the haying season. I also worked in the garden, but I never milked the cows! It was my father's conviction that women should never milk cows. He didn't believe it was safe for women to be around them.

I worked hard around the house too. I often babysat my two younger sisters and washed the laundry as well as tended to other household chores. During the summer, I helped a neighbor clean her house and babysat for others close by too.

While my parents were not Christians, they were good, hard working, moral people of high value. Two of my most cherished memories are Otis leading my father to the Lord before he died, and my mother receiving Christ as her Savior shortly after my father went to heaven. Growing up, we were blessed with the warmth of a good home, food on the table, sufficient clothes to wear and, most importantly, we knew we were loved.

My father was selectman for the town of Whitefield, a distinct honor which he held for over 20 years. He was well respected, being asked to serve as a pallbearer for many funerals in town. In the early 1960s, the two-room school building I attended was finally closed. My mom and another lady started the hot lunch program in the new consolidated school.

I was blessed with a dear neighbor who picked me up for Sunday School. For years, our little church next door to the school closed during the harsh winter months. We waited patiently many years for a full-time pastor. We loved the visiting pastors who would come in the summer months, preaching three times in one day in three different churches. In the winter months when our church was closed, God provided a faithful messenger for us – a widow lady who would take us to her home for Sunday School. There were always fun activities and Bible stories, and this, no doubt, was the beginning of my spiritual walk. This widow lady is indeed one of God's unsung heroes.

One summer in the early 1950s, we had a young man come to our church to be the youth director. He was in Bible college, and his father was the part-time pastor of our church, Whitefield Union Church. Our youth director took us to a youth rally in Alna, Maine, and this was pivotal in my life. I went forward to be saved at that rally. I remember it clearly, but in the years to follow, I was never discipled to grow in my faith. My parents refused to allow me to be baptized. It wasn't until I was married and expecting our first baby that I was finally baptized.

I attended the local elementary school in Kings Mills. The school consisted of first through eighth grades, no kindergarten. It was a two-story schoolhouse. Grades first through fourth were held on the first floor while fifth through eighth were on the second floor. These were the days of few conveniences. We dealt with no running water, no heat apart from a pot-bellied wood stove, and an attached outhouse. Some of the older boys, the teacher, or the bus driver was required to get the fire going on those cold Maine mornings, often 10-15 degrees below zero. For drinking water, we had to lug water from Union Hall up the road to the school. We did not even have paper cups; imagine no paper cups! We made cups for drinking water out of arithmetic paper. What is it they say, "Necessity is the mother of invention" … cups from arithmetic paper!

The school was located very close to the road with barely enough room to park a car between the road and the building. At the back of the school was a brook. The fire escape was old and rickety, so if the students ever had to evacuate, it would have collapsed as soon as the students stepped on it. We did not have a school bus for transportation but instead were transported in a station wagon. Looking back, I marvel how God kept us all safe as we crossed the road daily.

I loved the winters at this little school, and I recollect many days of great fun. The neighbor next to the school had a huge hill just tailor-made for sledding. We would go sledding every day at noon and often return on weekends too. In harsh winters, sometimes 10 degrees below zero, with the brook frozen behind the schoolhouse, we would spend many hours outdoors enjoying the winter months.

Winter was equally fun at home. Our family had a neighbor with a huge pond that would freeze over creating the perfect skating rink. We would burn old tires for warmth and light for our skating parties. None of this was against the law in those days; no environmentalist to petition against the smell and smoke. What great fun we had in those days!

One of my most cherished memories of Christmas was the year I received a pair of white ice skates. The thrill I experienced at opening that present to reveal those gleaming ice skates is as vivid today as that day many years ago. In those days we did not receive many gifts, but I loved and needed those ice skates.

Another fond memory was "the hanging of May baskets" in the month of May. What a thrill to receive the colorfully decorated basket full of candy! Half the fun was trying to catch the person who delivered the baskets. You see, someone would deliver the basket and run away to hide once they knocked on the door. This was such a delightful game for us kids. Everyone waited eagerly to see if they were going to be the next one to receive a basket. We lived in a world where children felt safe running up and down the roads with no fear of harm, even at night.

We enjoyed simple pleasure. We had no television, and most did not even have a telephone. We were not involved in drinking or smoking, and drugs were unheard of in those innocent days. However, I must admit, my friend and I did get caught stealing! My friend had an older sister with a boyfriend who gifted her with chocolates. What a temptation because, you see, we knew where she kept them. Every so often, we would sneak into her room and help ourselves to the beckoning chocolate sweets. We actually thought we were getting away with it. But alas, one day her sister was watching from the window as we were piling on the chocolates. It was summer, so the windows were open, and the next thing we heard was a booming voice shouting, "GET OUT OF MY CHOCOLATES!" We dropped them and ran, dreading the severe punishment we feared would accompany our "desperate crime." Her sister was very kind and merciful to us, but enjoyed teasing me about my "criminal act," even into my married years. Our lives were sheltered, and we knew little of desperate situations and unexplainable persecution, poverty, and horrors people faced around the world.

Attending school, my teacher for the upper grades was a close family friend. For that reason, I was often referred to as the "teacher's pet." She was "old school" and would read the Bible every day and pray for and with the class. She was fearless regarding discipline, hitting anyone who deserved it on the head with a ruler, snatching their hair, and even pounding their head against their desk. Her method of "ruling with an iron fist" worked well but would not be tolerated in today's permissive society. Teachers have been fired and even put in jail for less.

During the summer of 1953, a new family, John and Iva Goodwin, moved to our town. They had a son, Otis, and a daughter, Marion, who was away in nursing school. That fall when school started, I was in the eighth grade, and it seemed my life began to expand with a new awareness even though I was very shy. I am not sure I understood all of it and certainly had no idea what was ahead of me! Otis always told people that the first time he saw me, he knew he was going to marry me. I believe they call this "love at first sight." In a small village like ours, with few teens around, a shy little red-headed girl caught his eye. I actually enjoyed the attention but did not want anyone to know.

All the kids soon realized there was something brewing. We could not let our parents know, as we were very young. Our school teacher, Neota Grady, was in the dark until our Halloween party that fall when she noticed the attraction.

I graduated from the eighth grade from the Kings Mills Elementary School in 1954. My dad had graduated from this same school in 1925. Otis went on to Erskine Academy and later to Cony High School in Augusta, Maine, and I went on to attend Gardiner High School.

Otis' parents began attending my church, Whitefield Union Church, when they moved to town. Otis' mother was my Sunday School teacher. Once Otis got his driver's license, he would come to pick me up for Sunday School and church, and then I would spend the day with his family. Is it any wonder that I had perfect attendance in Sunday School? Otis' mother rewarded me with a beautiful white Bible – my very first. This very special, very sentimental Bible is the one I carried on my wedding day.

Like many, I enjoyed my high school years. Living in the country, I had to find a ride to get to school. My ride worked an 8-5 job in Augusta, so after school each day, I had to go to the city library and wait to be picked up for the ride home. It made for a long day, but I was able to do all my homework before I arrived home. You might say it was a blessing in disguise. This arrangement lasted all four years while I was in high school. Once I received my driver's license my senior year, I enjoyed the rare privilege of taking the family car to school. That was a special treat I did not take for granted. My studies were important to me, and I was elected to the National Honor Society my senior year. This honor brought me great joy and made my careful attention to my schoolwork worthwhile.

Otis and I dated throughout the first three years of high school. Our first date to the Pittston Fair was due, in part, to the fact that Otis was a hard worker. He always had a part-time job with funds for special activities. This meant we could go out to eat and go to movies, and his responsible nature allowed him use of the family car. We always doubled dated, and I certainly had a curfew.

One eventful memory was the night I was late beyond my curfew. I thought we had enough time to go see a movie and still have time to go to our favorite place to eat. We almost made it to my home when we met my father coming to look for me! When I got out of the car my father said to Otis, "We will have no more of this." We thought we were in big trouble, but we knew that my father meant what he said. There was no need for anything more to be said.

In the summer of 1957, between our junior and senior year, Otis joined the Air National Guard and went to Lackland Air Force Base in Texas for boot camp. At the end of the summer he came back to Maine for a brief visit with me. Next, he moved to California with his parents for his senior year of high school. He graduated from Mt. Miguel High School in 1958. I graduated from Gardiner High School and went to work for two dentists, Dr. Church and Dr. Cooper, who practiced in Gardiner. After graduation, Otis moved back to Maine, and we were married October 26, 1958. We had a lovely wedding in my home church which was located across the road from the elementary school we attended together in the eighth grade. In the transitory world we live in, these circumstances are more than rare today.

God's prophetic words in Isaiah thousands of years ago had the same divine implication on our lives in 1958 as it did when it was written in the eighth century. I could never have imagined how God would orchestrate and maneuver the plan for our lives in the years ahead. *My Incredible Journey* had just begun!

# 2

# A Little Boy's Story

Marvel not that I said unto thee, Ye must be born again.

John 3:7 KJV

Otis' dad, John Franklin Goodwin, was the first son of Archie and Annie Blaisdell Goodwin in Gardiner, and his only brother, Leon, joined the family a few years later to complete the family. John came from a close and loving middle-class family that had lived in this charming city for many generations.

John's family attended Free Baptist Church in Gardiner, and he was very involved in the youth ministry program.

John had a very easy-going spirit, and that followed him all his life. He was a great fisherman and proudly carried the card of the "State of Maine, Department of Inland Fisheries and Game, License to Trap in the Organized Territory" dated October 19, 1953. He and his brother had a very special and loving home life and were taught that family and faith were the foundation for a successful marriage and a growing family. They had a blessed relationship with their grandparents and cousins, and it was a testimony to their children when they started their own families.

In the meantime, hundreds of miles north of Gardiner in Stickney, New Brunswick, Canada, a young girl by the name of Iva Mae Cullens lived in deep poverty in a dysfunctional home with an abusive father. She would tell of times when she was going to school and the only food she had in her lunch box was a cold potato. She would go off by herself to eat so the other kids would not see her meager lunch.

She and her four siblings lived in a small shack with no running water and no electricity. Iva's mother was a godly woman but only knew bits and pieces of the Bible. She prayed often and taught her children to pray. When Iva was a young girl, she attended a Pentecostal church service and accepted Jesus as her Lord and Savior. It was in the month of February, so they cut a hole in the ice, and she was baptized.

Iva was 14 years old when her mother died, and she took on the responsibility of caring for the other children. Her father would take his anger out on her. Life was tough. Iva had family in Mars Hill, Maine, and when they heard of her mother's death they knew they needed to rescue Iva from the home. The family went to Canada, put Iva in the back of a wagon, covered her with a blanket, and took her to the United States. She was, therefore, brought illegally into the United States. She was an illegal alien. She became an American citizen February 9, 1956.

She lived with her grandmother in Mars Hill for three years until her grandmother died. Then she went to live with a cousin in Gardiner and worked as a housekeeper and nanny. After Iva began working for the family, they received a delivery from the local market. On that particular day, the delivery boy was John Goodwin and the young lady receiving the delivery was Iva Cullens. He thought she was cute, but she thought all men were like her father. Eventually he won her over, and they were married on March 30, 1930.

They went to live with his parents. Marion Augusta, their first child and only daughter, arrived on November 1, 1931, and their only son, Otis Shelborn, arrived on July 15, 1939. Otis was a sickly baby through his adolescence years. He was diagnosed with asthma and sleep was not a common lifestyle for him. In his formative years he experienced fairly good health, but in his late teen years he developed the serious health problem of colitis which increased in severity as time went on creating more health problems that followed him his entire life. This resulted in years of difficult surgeries and even times of near death.

Otis lived most of his formative years in Gardiner and Whitefield. He led the usual lifestyle of a young boy. He worked as the paper boy and enjoyed going fishing with his father and swimming at the Old Mill in the summer. He took saxophone lessons but never really focused on making it a priority in his life. He was, however, always eager to fix broken items – machines, furniture, or anything that was broken. This was in his DNA, and his motto in life was, "You never pay to have anything fixed."

This trait showed up very early in life as well as in the years to follow such as the time our daughter, Jana, needed her piano to be repaired. His mother tells the story of him fixing her sewing machine. Money was tight in those days, and his mother sewed the family clothing. Otis overheard his mother tell his father that the sewing machine needed repairs. One day as his mother was busy doing laundry, she realized he had been quiet for a long time. She came and found 6-year-old Otis sitting in a pile of sewing machine pieces all over the floor. He looked up at her and very proudly said, "I am fixing your sewing machine." Needless to say, his mother was devastated and quickly left the room before she did something drastic to her little son. Unlike the piano, the sewing machine was never the same.

His family was active in church, and they became lifelong friends with the pastor, Martin Storms, and his family. Rev. Storms was the pastor who married Otis and me in 1958. The pastor's son, Roger, became Otis' best friend. At the age of 12, in 1952, Otis went to Word of Life in Scroon Lake, New York for summer camp. He really enjoyed summer camp. His sister remembered that he kept calling home for more money. At the closing program during the big, traditional bonfire, Otis knew he needed to be saved, and he went forward to receive Jesus Christ as his Lord and Savior.

Otis was always working from his teens into adulthood. He always held some sort of a part-time job as a teen in the summer and winter months. When his family moved to Whitefield, he worked for a local farmer in the summer and winter. He enjoyed having money to buy his own clothes, and he had the funds to enjoy life when it came time to date and partake in all the activities that go along with teenage years. He enjoyed going camping with his friends and fishing too. In his junior year of high school, he went to work part time with The Great Atlantic and Pacific Tea Company (an American grocery store chain better known as A&P).

In the summer of 1957, he completed boot camp training at Lackland Air Force Base and was part of the inactive reserves. After boot camp he moved to California for his senior year in high school. His parents had moved there from Maine, along with his sister and her family. They had purchased a nursing home, and Otis worked in the nursing home during his last year of high school.

After his graduation he returned to Maine and again went to work for A&P, while I was working full time for a dental practice.

It was during his years at the A&P that he learned to be a meat cutter. This skill was a blessing many years down the road when we owned a supermarket because he was prepared to cut beef, deer, pigs, or whatever meat that needed to be dressed. But then there were also times we would go out for a steak dinner, and the cut of meat on his plate was not what he ordered. He would tell the waiter, "I know my beef, and this is not what I ordered." Otis loved his steak. Our children and grandchildren laugh about it now, but, at the time, they wanted to crawl under the table from embarrassment.

It was during this time in life that we started discussing our plans for the future. I said to him one day, "I think we should set a date for our wedding." He quickly agreed. Both our parents agreed on an October wedding, and we began a whirlwind of preparations for October 26, 1958. Otis had turned 19 that July, and I would turn 19 three days after our wedding.

The first item to attend to was buying our first vehicle. We searched and searched until we found "Honest John's" dealership. We were very proud of the 1955 green Ford, and it lasted us a number of years.

This was a special time for my mom and me as we worked together shopping for a wedding gown as well as dresses for my maid of honor, bridesmaids, and flower girl. It was exciting working on all the details that go into picking just the right fall colored flowers, planning the reception, and deciding on the wedding cake. Otis was responsible for the pictures since he worked with a man who was a photographer, and he scheduled the honeymoon too.

All the wheels had been set in motion for that special October day. The day we would become husband and wife and start our *Incredible Journey* together.

Otis was very proud of his heritage. What a privilege to be born into a family that had a godly heritage from generations past! It was his heart's desire and determination that we would do our very best, with the Lord as our guide, to ensure that we left a godly heritage to our future generations.

> The lines are fallen unto me in pleasant places; yea,
> I have a goodly heritage.
>
> Psalm 16:6 KJV

# 3

# Boy Marries Girl

> Tell ye your children of it, and let your children tell
> their children, and their children another generation.
> Joel 1:3 KJV

s I write our family's history, I pray that generations to come will see the godly heritage that was built from this day forth …

**October 26, 1958**

Months of planning, shopping, and bridal showers were behind us. The wedding invitations were mailed; beautiful fall flowers were arranged; and the bridal gown was purchased. The honeymoon was all planned, and the wedding rings were bought and engraved. Little did we know 49 years later our oldest grandson, Joshua Otis Bailey, would wear his grandfather's wedding ring when he married Becky

Wright! Otis' folks were not able to attend the wedding because they were living in California and owned a nursing home. This was a sad time, but we understood the circumstances. Otis' Aunt Ada and Uncle Leon Goodwin honored us by standing in for his parents.

Finally, the day arrived. There was standing room only at my childhood church, Whitefield Union Church. We had a beautiful reception in the Whitefield Union Hall (which is now on the National Register of Historic Places). The hall was crowded with many well-wishers. My mother and her friend made the beautiful and delicious wedding cake. We received many beautiful gifts, of which I still have several. We honeymooned in Quebec, Canada because Otis' heritage on his mother's side came from Canada.

When we returned from Canada we went back to work – Otis at the A&P and I at the dentist office. Our first apartment was on Highland Avenue in Gardiner. Our first Sunday as a young married couple, we started attending Winter Street Baptist Church in the same town.

During the first few months of going to Winter Street we made the decision that I needed to be baptized. This was a little complicated because I discovered that I was pregnant, but with the doctor's permission, I was baptized, and we joined the church. After we joined the church, we had a visit from a church member talking to us about pledging our tithes to the church. That was the beginning of our commitment to giving tithes and offerings to our local church.

When our baby girl, Kimberly Ann, was born she was added to the cradle roll at Winter Street Baptist Church. A few months after Kim was born, Otis was offered an assistant manager position at the A&P in Dexter, Maine. Little did we realize that we were about to embark on a major health rollercoaster that would follow us through our journey of life until the day Otis died.

Otis came home one day and said that he had just come from the doctor's office. He had not mentioned anything to me about having any health problems recently. After several tests he was diagnosed with mucous colitis. There was no cure, and it was a chronic disease.

Life became quite challenging. Money was very tight as I didn't work with a new baby. The medication was expensive, and he had to be very careful with his diet. Our doctor bills were piling up, and Otis was having a difficult time controlling the colitis. He had to be hospitalized several times.

He was working long hours, and we did not have family close by for support. Otis' parents were still in California, and my parents were four hours away. I developed asthma and was struggling with that too during this time. Finally, after a couple of years, we decided we needed to move back home with my parents. In the meantime, I became pregnant with our daughter, Julie Louise.

Finally, life began to settle down. We were able to build a new home next to my parents, and Otis went to work for our local grocer. (Years later we purchased this store.) Otis was still struggling with his health. Due to our large medical expenses, Otis had to change jobs in order to obtain health insurance, and I went back to work full time.

Julie Louise was born and was a joy to our family. We had two beautiful daughters, and they were growing and healthy.

Otis' parents moved back home from California and purchased a home in Jefferson. It was wonderful to have them close by, and they were a tremendous support for us. The home they purchased had lake frontage, enabling us to go camping, swimming, and fishing. We purchased a boat and had a wonderful time water skiing. We spent many long hours with family and friends at the lake. Otis was an avid water skier on one ski! However, it took a whole summer being dragged all over the lake for me to be able to get up on two skis the last day of summer. Otis worked hard, and we played hard.

You always hear people tell their bear story; well, I have one to tell too! We always went camping over Labor Day weekend.

This one particular time we went to Baxter State Park in northern Maine. Otis' sister and her family were with us. We arrived at the campground late on Friday night. We had our sleeping bags and stayed in a three-sided lean-to. Otis' brother-in-law had a pickup truck with all our supplies in the back, including a big insulated box where we kept our perishable items. After getting settled for the night, I was sleeping with one eye open. I heard a noise, sat up straight, and looked right into the face of a bear. I poked Otis and whispered, "Quick! Wake up! There is a bear in front of our lean-to!"

He responded, "Keep quiet and don't move," I obeyed, but my heart must have been pounding loud enough for the bear to hear it. Finally, after a few minutes, the bear moved along, got up into the truck body and tried to get into the insulated box without success. Needless to say, I didn't go back to sleep that night.

The next morning we were cooking breakfast over the campfire and who should come loping along but the bear – just like he owned the place. By this time people were up moving around. The game wardens came by and said they were going to anesthetize the bear and take him further into the woods on the other side of the park.

After breakfast, we took the kids down to the rocks and water falls, and we were gone about three hours. When we returned to our campsite, we discovered that the bear had returned and enjoyed a nap in my brother-in-law's lean-to; it was covered with dirt and bear hair. The bear also tore down a tent near our site, evidently looking for food. Unfortunately, the wardens ended up killing the bear because it was becoming too friendly, and they were afraid it would attack someone. End of the bear story!

When winter began it was snowmobiling time. We went to Canada with our snowmobile and visited with Otis' aunt and uncle. Otis went snowmobiling all weekend. We came home, and soon he was in total misery and extreme pain. We ended up in the emergency room, and, at first, the doctor thought he had an obstruction.

But praise the Lord it ended up only being a kink in the bowel that worked itself out. Once again, the Lord raised him up.

Otis loved ice fishing, and once when he was up in Moosehead Lake in northern Maine, he caught a four-pound brook trout. It was quite the trophy. We put it in our freezer, and I took it to a taxidermist and had it mounted. Our grandson and avid sportsman, Corey, has that trophy in his home now.

Life was never dull in the Goodwin house! Our family was coming home late one night after bowling. It was pouring rain when suddenly Otis jammed on the brakes and jumped out of the car. He had hit something and went to check it out. He came rushing back trying to find something in the back of the car – a box or bag or anything. Finally, he returned with something in his hand and threw it in the back of the station wagon, and we went on home. I asked, "What did you put in that box?" He said, "I don't know." When we arrived home, we discovered it was a dead mink – a good sized one too with large teeth. I was very thankful that it died on impact and was not just stunned while in our station wagon! Corey now has this trophy in his home also. These two trophies were Otis' pride and joy!

Otis had his ups and downs periodically with his health, but we were enjoying our family and church. We were busy in the church and in the community. Otis was a volunteer fireman, and I was involved with the Helping Hand Society at church.

We always enjoyed our town's annual Fourth of July celebration. We enjoyed the parade, the greased pig, the greased pole, the auction, bingo, lots of food, and the dance that closed out the day's activities. Otis and I loved to dance, and he was quite the dancer. We enjoyed dancing until God called us into the ministry. As you know dancing is not setting a good role model for Baptist churchgoers, especially if you are in full-time ministry. Years later Otis would say, "When I get to heaven and I find out that dancing was okay, I am going to be very upset!"

As our girls were growing up, we tried very hard to teach them about godly family life and that they were part of our family unit. We used to have family council meetings periodically. If there was an issue that needed addressing, a family vacation to plan, or whatever topic that needed the attention of our entire family, we would post a notice on each bedroom door with the time and date of the meeting and that attendance was required. We had many conversations – some difficult, some happy, and many that were blessings.

Otis' health was deteriorating, but he always worked hard and never missed a day of work. Now he had been diagnosed with ulcerated colitis, and I had to give him daily injections of steroids. This went on for a couple of years when one day I received a call that he had collapsed on his job, and they had taken him to the hospital in Augusta. When I arrived, the doctor examining him said he needed to be transferred to Waterville, as he needed more expert care than they were able to provide for him. His condition was so bad that the doctors said surgery was needed and there was no other choice.

So, on July 26, 1968, at the age of 28, he had colorectal surgery and ended up with an ileostomy. This would be permanent. He was in intensive care for 10 days with no sign of recovering from the surgery. Finally, he began to respond and gain strength, and he started recovering quickly.

This was not an easy surgery for a young man to cope with emotionally. Only by God's grace did he accept the situation, due to the fact he felt better than he had for several years. For the first time in years he was not on any medication or injections of steroids. The cost of his medication had been so high that his mother would give us her paycheck so we could afford it.

The doctor told him at discharge that he could do anything that he felt like doing. I don't think the doctor really knew Otis, because on Labor Day he was determined that he was going to water ski! Much to my dismay, he kept repeating what the doctor said each time I objected. So he did take a quick trip around the lake and was very pleased with his accomplishment and that there were no ill effects. Thank the Lord!

Life began to move forward in a new light. Otis was always looking for new adventures. We began buying different types of property. At one time we owned three apartment houses and even a car wash. Each was a tremendous headache and responsibility.

Business-wise we were very busy and family-wise God gave us a BIG surprise. I was pregnant with our third child. Our two oldest girls were 11 and 13 when Jana Lubell was born. Our family was truly complete. Otis was very proud of his three daughters and never once wished for a son. Although many years later God gave us five precious grandsons.

Life was moving along. Otis was working as a salesman, and his health was quite good. Our girls were growing and were a tremendous blessing to our whole family.

But one of the most bittersweet times in my life was about to happen. My dad was taken to the Augusta hospital with chest pains and was immediately transferred to a hospital in Portland, Maine for heart surgery which he never recovered from. The angels carried him to heaven on December 6, 1972. A few days prior to his death, Otis led him to the Lord. So I have the comfort and peace of knowing that one day I will see him again. He was 62 years old. This was an extremely difficult time for my mother, and now I had an added responsibility of helping to care for her. Our new baby girl was just six months old.

Otis did not let any grass grow under his feet, so in 1974 we added another major responsibility to our life. We purchased the country store where Otis had worked a few years earlier. Goodwin's Country Market was in business along with our three apartment houses.

This business was a challenge to our marriage and family. One blessing was that Otis' father came and worked in the office of the store doing all the accounting and bookkeeping. Kim was in high school, so she worked in the store to earn money. But it was challenging too. We eventually found ourselves in need of an attack dog! He really was an attack dog – trained to attack on demand. The store had had several break-ins or attempted break-ins. We had one incident where the burglar got as far as the meat counter and tried to bribe the dog with a piece of meat, but it didn't work. We found nothing missing – only an open window!

Otis and I had several clashes over how things were to be run, until one day Otis came home in the middle of the day and said, "I am going to sell the store." I responded with "Why?" He replied, "The store is going to ruin our marriage." So, I decided there had to be one boss, and I backed off and let him run the business. It was a demanding business, but we did have some good times during this time too. During Kim's senior year, Otis planned a secret trip to take our family to Walt Disney World before Kim went away to college. It was a memorable time for our family.

When we bought the store, it was necessary to move from our three-bedroom home to a three-bedroom trailer next door to the store. It was a mixed blessing. We were close to the store, but five people and a dog living in a small space had its moments.

Also, another change for our family was that Otis and I decided we needed to change churches. Leaving the church I grew up in to attend a church close to our new home was a big challenge. Later in our life, this church, Calvary Bible Baptist Church, became our sending church when we went into full-time missions. Still to this day they are our sending church, and this is the church my two oldest girls and their families attend.

During these years at the store and our new church, we were very involved with the different ministries. One major undertaking was the construction of the new church building. Years earlier the original church building burned down. The church owned a parsonage with an attached barn, and they renovated the barn into a temporary church sanctuary. Otis was the general foreman for the construction of the new church building. This took much time away from the store and family. He worked every night and many hours in the day on the building. Finally, a beautiful new church building was completed, and it is a light in the community to this day.

During these few challenging years at the store and after increased involvement in the church, the Lord began working on Otis' heart about full-time ministry. One day in 1977, Otis had been outside chopping wood when he came and said, "I think the Lord will have us go to school and become a pastor." There were several churches in Maine that were looking for a pastor at that time, and Otis kept saying Nova Scotia might be the place we would go. Well that was not on my radar at that moment. Kimberly was in her first year of college, Julie was in a Christian high school, and Jana was in kindergarten. (Kim started college the same day that Jana started kindergarten. We took Kim to Boston, Massachusetts, and Julie took Jana to her first day of school. It was a family affair!)

We were in an overwhelming situation with the apartment houses, the store, our family situation, and three daughters ranging from college to kindergarten. Money was tight! Our properties were not doing well because we had renters who were not paying their rent. It all seemed impossible. Otis was determined that the Lord would have us pack up and go back to school. The Sounds of Liberty from Liberty Baptist College (now Liberty University) in Lynchburg, Virginia had been at a local church a few months earlier, so Otis decided this was where he would go to college even though we had been out of high school for 20 years.

We did not receive any encouragement from our friends or family. Otis' mother was very upset we were taking her grandchildren to Virginia. On top of everything and to make matters more interesting, I discovered I was pregnant again. I was having a difficult pregnancy, so the doctor put me on bed rest.

So here we were in the process of selling our businesses and moving from Maine to Virginia while our family was upset, one daughter was in college, one was in high school, one just going into the first grade, and I was on bed rest expecting another baby. The girls were doing the packing. It was a stressful and very emotional time, as I was not able to carry the baby to full term.

Finally, after many months of planning, on August 1, 1978 we gathered at the church where many of our friends came to pray for us and see us off. There were many tears. Kim had decided she would not go back to Boston for college, but instead go to the community college in Lynchburg and live at home. High school was a very difficult time for Julie to leave her friends. Jana was young enough to want to just be with her mom and dad, but old enough to realize she would be away from grandparents. My mother went to live with her sister, and my two sisters took responsibility for her. However, there were times when my mother would live in our home in Virginia too. Otis had already flown to Lynchburg to register for college and enroll Julie and Jana in Lynchburg Christian Academy as well as rent a house. He even applied for a job with the campus security at Liberty which he had the entire time we were in Lynchburg.

It was a very daunting situation, but Otis was convinced this was what the Lord would have us do. Our life as we had known it was fast coming to an end. I felt like Sarai from the Bible when Abram told her to pack up and move. I knew where we were going, but I had no idea what we would run up against the day that we rolled out of Maine in that Ryder moving truck with our three girls and dog. We were moving a thousand miles away. We literally had no money after getting out from under our businesses and home. There was no money for Otis and Kim's college, nor for Julie and Jana's Christian school. I knew I would have to go to work, but since I did not go to college, I wasn't sure just what I could do.

It was a long trip with the moving truck and our family, however we finally reached our new home after 20 hours of travel arriving late at night in the very hot Virginia summer heat. We were all tired, scared, stressed, and full of anticipation and apprehension concerning what was ahead for us as a family.

# 4

## Provisions

> It is of the Lord's mercies that we are not consumed, because his compassions fail not. They are new every morning: great is thy faithfulness.
> Lamentations 3:22-23 KJV

**August 1978**

It was by God's faithfulness and His mercies every morning that we were not consumed by the tasks waiting for us as we moved forward with this new chapter in our family. We hit the ground running, so to speak. We didn't have much time to get settled in our new home we were renting. It was a delightful home in the countryside of Monroe, Virginia.

Otis began his new job working security for Liberty Baptist College. I found a job working at a local department store. Kim began classes at Virginia Community College. Julie and Jana were enrolled at Lynchburg Christian Academy.

After 20 years out of high school, Otis went to college. He was taking a full load of classes – 18 hours – and working full time at Liberty along with a part-time job as a car salesman. I was working full time and taking classes at the community college; I had to learn to type so I would be able to type Otis' papers. Needless to say, our plate was full!

During this time, we were about to begin another chapter in our lives. Kim and Randy Bailey had been dating during her first year of college. As Otis and I were about to start our first year of college, they came to us for permission to be married that fall. This was quite overwhelming to say the least. We needed a family council meeting in a hurry! After we discussed the pros and cons, they decided to wait until June 1979 for the wedding. So now we had a wedding to plan too!

It soon became apparent that we lived too far away from the schools and work, so we moved from our beautiful countryside home into a rented single-family home on Candlers Mountain just above the college.

Otis focused his degree on a pastoral major. Our plans – but not the Lord's – were to go back to Maine or even Nova Scotia to fill a pulpit in a local community. He had not been in school very long when the mission's pastor at Liberty, Rosco Brewer, preached on a mission's driven theme about going into all the world. That day is still fresh in my mind when Otis came home and said, "I think that the Lord would have us go into missions." This was the beginning of our *Incredible Journey* going into all the world.

I was open to the Lord's leading, and we began praying for the Lord's will. Life was busy. Otis chose bus ministry for his Christian service. That was a rewarding ministry, but one that was very time consuming. Saturday mornings were meetings and visitation. God blessed our labor for two years. The ministry grew, and we ended up with two bus routes. His second Christian service was serving in a chaplain capacity at the prison in Chatham, Virginia. Along with a full load of classes and Christian service, Otis started a different part-time job at a Food Lion grocery store. He would go days with little sleep.

During his second semester, Dr. Lee Bruckner was the professor in one of Otis' mission classes at Liberty. Before every class began, they prayed for China. During this time God spoke to Otis' heart, and he began to realize that the land of China was on our radar even though China was closed at this time. The door was not opened to missionaries, but that did not stop Otis' idea of going to China one day. When he came home that day and said, "We are going to work in China," I didn't know what to say. It was over and above my imagination.

The Lord guided us through the first year of college. We were overwhelmed financially with Christian school and college tuition. We had signed a commitment form with Thomas Road Baptist Church that we would tithe. Thankfully we were given a discount on Julie and Jana's tuition, and Kim was accepted into a work study program, so these were truly blessings. Otis finished his first year of college well and passed all his courses. Julie and Jana had adjusted quite nicely to a new family life. I had changed jobs and was now working for our church in the transportation department. I was the dispatcher for all the buses and vehicles for the entire ministry.

On June 30, 1979, Kim and Randy were married at Calvary Bible Baptist Church, our home church in North Whitefield, Maine. It was a beautiful wedding, and what a joy to see her walking down the aisle on the arm of her dad, beautifully dressed in my wedding gown. Randy was in the Air Force, and she had completed her second year of college at the community college. They settled down in South Carolina where Randy was stationed.

When Otis started his second year at Liberty, he changed from a pastoral major to a cross cultural major. He told everyone that one day he was going to work in China. People told him "no way" since China was closed. He was convinced that one day he would realize his dream of standing on the Great Wall in China. Otis continued his rigorous schedule. I was now attending Liberty part time and working full time. Julie had started work at Wendy's restaurant part time, and on the nights that she had to work until closing, I would have to wake Jana up and go pick Julie up from work in the wee hours of the morning. As time went on, we were able to purchase a car for Julie, so life became easier.

During the second and third years of college, life was a challenge and money was tight, but at the same time, we were learning to depend on God. We had no choice. Otis fasted and prayed one day a week, and our faith grew. We had been used to having the inventory of our grocery store in Maine at our disposal. Whatever we wanted to eat it was at our fingertips. The day we left for school that all changed. There were times we had to wait for payday to buy groceries for dinner. One of the benefits of working for Food Lion was that Otis was given broken bags of flour, dented cans, and day-old bakery items. We had friends who were in the same situation, and we were able to share our bounty with them. We also got into a financial difficulty with the amount of taxes we owed the Internal Revenue Service and were having a difficult time paying our taxes. What a stressful day when we discovered the IRS had garnished our paychecks just before payday. Only by God's grace were we able to pay off what we owed the government without having to borrow any money.

On January 5, 1981, we became grandparents! Our first grandchild, Joshua Otis Bailey, was born, and what a joy he was and has always been throughout the years. Kim and Randy were still in South Carolina, so we were able to see this precious gift from God from time to time.

Finally, we had reached a milestone, and Otis was beginning his senior year at Liberty. He had done very well and had passed all his courses, completed his Christian service, and managed to be a husband, father and now a grandfather while working strenuous hours. He became overwhelmed with all that was on his plate, so he decided to give up his part-time job. He often said he should have done it sooner because the Lord provided for us even when he only had one job.

Julie was about to make a change in life. She decided she wanted to move back to Maine and live with Otis' sister. During this time, she began to build a relationship with Glen Bailey – yes, the brother of Randy. Now we were down to just Jana living at home.

During our last year at Liberty we had major decisions that needed to be reached. It was a very busy time for me, as I was now attending Liberty full time and continued to work full time in the transportation department. Otis and I had both a 7 a.m. and evening classes together. I had a very nice neighbor who would care for Jana in the evenings when I had class. Otis was always late for our 7 a.m. class, because, at this time, he was working the command post for Liberty security at the Old Time Gospel Hour facility. A couple of years prior he worked security at Dr. Falwell's home. He always worked the late shift, and by working the radio command post he was able to study. I would take notes during our class time, and he would study my notes. He always received a better grade on tests than I did even though he studied from my notes. I didn't really do that well on my tests, but I did pass all my classes. One of my professors worked with Otis on security, and I think that he felt sorry for me.

During our final year at Liberty, it was exciting to see the end of our college years knowing we were on the threshold of a new beginning on our *Incredible Journey*. We were convinced God had His hand on us, and He had plans for us. What we needed to do was put our hands to the plow and move forward. During that previous year we started searching for a mission organization we could join to pursue what God was calling us to do – working with the

Chinese people. We had thought we might go to Hong Kong since China was still closed to the world, but, at the moment, we had to decide what we were going to do immediately after graduation.

Calvary Bible Baptist Church in North Whitefield and our pastor there, Ken Dutille, were discussing the possibility of us coming back home to do an internship there. The final decision came just before graduation, and we had faith it would be a positive relationship toward beginning our next step in ministry.

Finally, the BIG day arrived! It was graduation time. Otis was about to receive his diploma in cross cultural ministry, and he accomplished it in four years. What a challenging adventure and journey we had experienced. We experienced God's blessings over and over and grew in faith. We worked hard and saw the miracles of God over and over. We never took a vacation except to go to Maine for Kim's wedding and to travel to South Carolina a few times to see our baby Joshua. With so few days off, it seemed as if days ran together. God gave us the energy and stamina to keep going.

I knew when Otis came to me that day long ago and told me God had really spoken to him about going back to school that our lives would never be the same. Then a few months later when we were in school and he felt that the Lord would have us to go into missions … and then yet a few years later when he felt the Lord call us into ministry in southeast Asia … I was overwhelmed by all of this. It was beyond my imagination how this was all going to take place.

I was asked by a pastor one time what stressed me out, and I replied, "When my husband came to me and said 'Roxann, God has given me a vision.'" I never knew what to expect. It was not easy to embark on this journey. It was a continuing growing in faith process. It was totally changing our family and lifestyle as we knew it. It was going into the unknown.

I knew the Lord would not lead my husband and me in two different directions. I knew the responsibility of moving forward to a life the Lord had for us would not work if I was not in agreement with my husband. I knew I needed to follow Otis' leadership. That didn't mean I didn't have an input. Together we were able to move forward with the determination that, prayerfully and with the Lord's guidance, He would use us in a way we could never have imagined. It was a lot of hard work with many challenges, but it held many blessings too.

Otis always said that the day he graduated he was going to have the Ryder moving truck loaded and running to take us to the next chapter in life. We were leaving a life behind that we never could have imagined we would be able to accomplish but carried with us the blessings we received from God. It was a life-changing experience. One that I did not want to do again!

When we looked back over those years, it was only by God's grace that we survived emotionally, physically, and financially. We came home with not one cent of student loans!

We were living examples that God's faithfulness is new every morning.

# Stepping Out in Faith

> Ask of me, and I shall give thee the heathen for thine inheritance, and the uttermost parts of the earth for thy possession.
>
> Psalm 2:8 KJV

God had brought us through an amazing chapter in our lives. We had finished the course of preparing to move forward with our goals. Otis had finished his college course. Our family was expanding; God gave us two more grandsons – Randall Lee and Corey Elliott. Now we were preparing for the next step in serving the Lord in missions.

In May of 1982, as soon as Otis graduated and Jana finished the fourth grade, we moved back to Maine. Calvary Bible Baptist Church had put Otis on staff to do our internship.

Julie and Glen were preparing to get married that June. The day finally arrived, and she was beautiful walking down the aisle wearing my wedding dress and holding her dad's arm. The wedding took place at our church, Calvary Bible Baptist Church. Glen and Julie settled down in Glen's family home in Jefferson, Maine. Both our older daughters were married and living nearby. We almost had an empty nest.

Let me explain about the history of our new home. The first church building in North Whitefield had burned down several years prior to our going to school. The church owned a large home with an attached barn, so they renovated the barn for a church facility while they planned for and built the new church building. This is the church building Otis had worked on years prior as the foreman. After the new building was completed, they renovated the barn into an apartment.

When we came back from college we lived in the apartment. It had two bedrooms and a wood stove in the center of the living room but no central heat and no insulation. By this time, the church had sold the property to our daughter, Kim, and her husband, Randy.

As you can imagine, it was a struggle to keep warm. Otis used to say we had a "back up heating system." We had to back up to the stove to keep warm! During a snow storm, we would have snow coming into our clothes closet in our bedroom. When we started doing our deputation travels, everything would be frozen when we arrived home.

The church paid our rent, our light bill, and gave Otis $100 a week salary. He went to work for the Town of Whitefield driving a school bus route, so that gave us some additional income plus health insurance. He had many jobs at the church – youth leader, choir director, mission team leader, preaching when needed, etc. I was working as well. A local church ran a Christian school in our church basement for two years, and I was the school secretary.

Our family was growing. Julie and Glen presented us with another beautiful grandson, Glen Michael. He arrived just before Christmas in 1983. God had been good to us giving us three daughters, and now we were enjoying having grandsons. A couple years later, Glen and Julie gave us another blessing. Andrew John was born. What a blessing our five grandsons have been to us over the years.

Once we got settled working in the church, we started searching for a mission organization. We did not realize the process involved. After a year we finally decided on an old established organization. We started going through an extensive application process which included psychological testing, aptitude testing, qualifications, and personality tests. It seemed endless and took nearly a year; we were already two years out of college. We decided two years was a good length of time to serve an internship.

We waited patiently for this board to finally give us a response to our application, and we received it on Memorial Day weekend in 1984. The answer was not what we expected; they had rejected us.

It was devastating news as Otis was convinced we would be accepted. I had had an uneasy feeling and was not really surprised. So, here we were finishing our internship, and we had no mission organization to join. They sent us a letter explaining the reasons we were not approved for their organization. They said we were too old – we were 42 years old – and that we would have difficulty learning a foreign language. Also, as a result of our testing, it showed we both had very independent spirits, and they thought we would not fit well in their highly organized and structured board.

Finally, after we had time to gather our thoughts and after much prayer, we were put in touch with another organization. This experience was a whirlwind from day one. The director invited us to a two-week long candidate school that was scheduled to begin in just two weeks. From there, Otis would leave from Washington D.C. for China. He would travel in China with Dr. and Mrs. Lee Bruckner, one of his professors from Liberty. Otis would be studying the Chinese language and touring the country. His dream to walk on the Great Wall would be realized, all in a time frame of four weeks!

It was one miracle after another to prepare Otis to go to China. First of all, he did not have a passport. One of the ladies in our church kept saying, "If you get your passport, everything else will fall into place." So, he and Jana made a father-daughter trip to Boston to apply for his passport. He did not have any proof that he needed a passport immediately because we hadn't had the funds to purchase his airline ticket yet. It was summer time, and since Otis drove school buses as a second job and I worked for a Christian school, our summer income was cut drastically.

When he arrived at the passport agency in Boston, he prayed he would get just the right agent who would take him through the entire process to receive his passport that day. Well, God surely was saying "You are on the right track." After all the forms were processed, the agent told him to come back in two hours, and the passport would be ready!

Proverbs 11:14 says "Where no counsel is, the people fall: but in the multitude of counsellors there is safety." Otis was always a great believer in this verse. As soon as he came back from Boston, he called several local pastors and friends together for a meeting that afternoon at our church and explained all that was taking place. Some of the pastors were not quite sure if we were doing the right thing, and many of our friends were excited. Needless to say, there was a mixed response. Pastor Lester Black of Richmond Corner Baptist Church in Richmond, Maine was one of the pastors who attended. During the discussion, Pastor Black asked Otis if he was sure this was what the Lord would have him to do. Otis replied, "I am sure," and Pastor Black said, "Go for it."

*Stepping Out In Faith*

We were in a state of anticipation. We were scared, nervous, and on an emotional roller coaster. How would we ever manage such an enormous task of preparing for Otis to go to China in a matter of days? We had no money and had no idea how we would get the funds needed. We needed $4,000 for candidate school alone plus funds for Otis' airfare to China, seven weeks of study at East China Normal University, a country tour after the language school, and miscellaneous expenses.

Well, it didn't take the Lord long to begin providing. The same night of the meeting that Otis had with the group of men, we were having a high school graduation at our church. Pastor Black had several students from his church in the graduating class, and when he came to the graduation that night, he gave Otis a $100 check, our first gift for the trip. Next, a business friend told us he was going to pay for the airline ticket to China. Another friend told Otis to meet him at lunch time at a local men's store, and when Otis arrived, our friend told the clerk to outfit Otis because he was going to China for the summer. Our church gave us a love offering, and one friend gave me a summer pass to the state park to help entertain Jana.

It was just amazing to see how the Lord provided. We soon were on our way to Washington Bible College near Washington D.C. Along the way, we took Julie and baby Michael, who was just a few months old, to visit friends in Lynchburg, then she would travel back to Maine with me after I dropped Otis off at the Washington National Airport. We arrived in Lynchburg around 8 p.m. We were driving down the main highway in Lynchburg when all of a sudden, a car came up behind us and started blinking its headlights, tooting the horn, and tailing our car. Otis pulled into a mall parking lot, and this car came up beside us. A young man jumped out, and we recognized this guy that Otis went to college with.

Dan Proctor was excited and said, "Otis I knew that was you when I saw the Maine license plate." They were both excited to see one another. We shared that Otis was getting ready to go to China, and Dan said they were preparing to go to Australia. Dan insisted that we come by their home that very moment to see Kim and to go over all the plans for China. Before we left, Dan and Kim collected all the cash they had and gave it to Otis. We were only lacking less than $100, and they gave us $100 that night. God is in control. What an encouragement to an unbelievable story. (Several years later Otis was able to visit with Kim and Dan in Australia.) The next day we were off to candidate school for two weeks, and we were accepted.

After we finished candidate school on June 16, 1984, we went directly to Washington National Airport. I still remember the moment I said goodbye to Otis in the airport parking lot. Little did I realize that this would be just the beginning of many times saying goodbye at airports.

Our whole world had turned upside down. We had no idea what we were doing or what was going to happen. I left to drive back to Virginia to pick up Julie and then on to Maine; it was my first time driving in Washington D.C. Otis was about to board a plane, alone, as the team had gone on before him, and fly halfway around the world with no idea what the Lord had in store for him. He would be gone for seven weeks total. These were the days of no email, no cell phones, or fax machines. The only way to communicate was through the United States and Chinese postal systems.

I wrote a letter every day to keep him updated on all that was going on at home; and after he had been in China for a few days, he went to the college post office every day to see if he had received a letter from me. He was getting desperate to know what was happening at home. All the clerks at the post office knew him by name and waited for him to come to the post office each day.

He told the Lord that if he didn't receive a letter soon, he was going home. Finally, after two weeks, he once again took his daily walk to the post office, and when he arrived the clerks all smiled and clapped their hands when they saw him. He had received a stack of letters.

The study was very intense, and he worked hard. He received his diploma and passed the course. I was back home worrying and praying with no idea what was going on with Otis in China. Little did I know that the Lord was shaping and developing a ministry for us that would endure and become a vital ministry for years to come … ministry that was unique and non-conventional … ministry that was not accepted by the mission board, as we discovered later, or with old established mission organizations. This was a new concept – to reach the restricted access countries of Southeast Asia with the gospel of Jesus Christ by working with national pastors in these countries.

The country of China had recently endured the Cultural Revolution in which communism was initiated. It was a very dark period for Chinese Christians, and it had a very negative impact on believers. Religious activities were effectively banned. Believers were arrested and sometimes tortured for their faith. Bibles were destroyed, Bible schools were closed, and churches and homes were looted. Thousands of believers were imprisoned for many years. This was the beginning of the house church movement … the underground church.

Dr. Bruckner had traveled to China several times, and he had made some contacts with underground pastors. Through these contacts, arrangements were made for Otis and Dr. Bruckner, along with a translator, to go to the home of an underground pastor. They went late at night walking through dark alleys and taking time to make sure they were not followed. They finally arrived at the home of an underground pastor and there with him was another pastor visiting in the home.

As they were there, there was an unexpected knock on the door. Everyone was startled and really quite afraid, especially the wife of the home. Anticipating it was the police, they put Otis and Dr.

Bruckner in a room and closed the door. When the pastor opened the door, he was relieved to see the friendly face of another underground pastor. The new arrival told the group that, "The Lord told him to come to this home tonight because there were people there that he needed to meet."

Otis was overwhelmed with the circumstances that were about to take place but knew that God had an amazing plan for our lives. After several hours of listening to the testimonies of these pastors, he realized what each of them had gone through for the Lord Jesus Christ. They told what it was like being in prison 20-25 years during the Cultural Revolution. The Christians had no Bibles; all the Bibles had been burnt and seminaries were closed during this terrible time in China. One pastor told how when he was set free, he went home to see his wife for the first time in 20 years. They hardly recognized one another.

It was during this meeting that Otis had the opportunity to talk to these godly men who had suffered way beyond our imagination and to still see the desire in their hearts to serve the Lord under immense persecution. Otis knew that the Lord had an unusual opportunity for him, and that he had to seize that open door.

So, as the night progressed Otis interviewed these men saying, "I want to serve you. I want to have a ministry that will come alongside of you and give you the tools to enable you to reach China for the Lord's kingdom. What can I do? I cannot come and live in China. It is not allowed. What can I do while living in America to help you to evangelize China?"

As these men began to share the needs they had, a new ministry was conceived. The needs were great. They had no money; they had no Bibles; they had no Christian literature; and they needed prayer support. They felt as if no one in the outside world knew of their plight.

One of the greatest blessings during this trip was the opportunity the team had to visit Wang Ming Da and his wife. Wang Ming

Da was in prison for 25 years during the Cultural Revolution and was one of the founders of the house church movement. He and his wife were along in years and shared with the team what went on during those terrible years of persecution in China. When we looked back on this trip and digested all the Lord had opened Otis' eyes to see – the needs and the vision and the concept of a ministry – it was beyond our comprehension.

Otis always dreamed of walking on the Great Wall of China. This was another blessing on top of so many others that resulted from this trip. But the greater blessing was that Otis was beginning to see the needs of these precious men and the church in China. Now what were we going to do about it?

Finally, after seven weeks in China, he arrived home with his head full of plans to move forward on what we knew – without a doubt – were the plans God had for us and for the future ministry.

I have attached a summary that Otis wrote concerning his first impression on what was about to take place after this first trip to China. He quickly realized something greater was about to happen far beyond studying the Chinese language.

*August 3, 1984*

*On June 16, 1984, I left Washington National Airport for a seven week stay in China. The flight to Shanghai, China was very long and lonely. On June 18, I arrived in Shanghai at 2:30 p.m. after a 34-hour trip. I was met at the airport by Dr. Bruckner, and we then went to the campus of East China Normal University. My first impression of China was that everything was so different.*

*On June 19, I was placed in the beginner's class of the Chinese language. Classes did not start until June 20.*

*The university had a party for us in the afternoon, and we met our teachers. One of our instructors spoke very little English which made it very difficult for me.*

*As classes began, I found myself involved in many other details of the trip and also found out that this was going to interfere with my studies. I decided that these other details were also very important to my future and made the decision to do as well as possible with the language class and also visit as much as possible.*

*I came to China to try to find ways by which I could aid the Chinese Christian church and at the same time decide, with the help of God, where and what He would have me to do for a ministry.*

*While in China I was able to talk to several house church leaders as well as pastors of the government run church organization. As I questioned these church leaders, I learned that there are many problems within the Chinese church. The split church situation between government and house churches is a huge problem. The government church is controlled, and the house churches seem to be lacking in any organization at all. I do believe while the government church is truly an arm of the government, that it does serve as a refuge for many Christians. It provides them with a place of worship and prayer, plus an opportunity to hear the Word of God expounded upon. This will provide for the growth of the saved Christians. I do not believe that unbelieving people could get saved in the government church without the help of another established Christian.*

*Within the house church movement, as I understand it, there seems to be a total lack of any organization at all. The group seems to consist of close family members only, although there are large house churches. The group meets at different times during the week and at different places. The object always seems to be to worship and maybe lacks in Bible growth. This I cannot say for sure. I do believe that the unsaved can truly hear the Word of God and be saved within the house church movement. Therefore, the hope for China and church growth seems to be with the house church movement.*

*There seemed to be a lack of enthusiasm within the government church, where within the house church there seemed to abound a real spirit of enthusiasm for the Lord Jesus Christ. I believe this is very important. Maybe a better way to express it would be to say the government church has a very inward nature, whereas the house church is outgoing towards only a very few.*

*The house church movement's biggest problem is that it is operational against the will of the government. This makes the spreading of the gospel a very slow job.*

*Every church leader I spoke to said, with great emphasis, that the biggest help that can be given to the church in China is prayer. "Pray for the Church in China."*

*Evangelism inside China by westerners is a very slow and frustrating ordeal. You have to be very careful. Throughout our stay in China I know of only four decisions for Christ by the eight members of our team. I do believe much seed was planted for future harvest.*

*My Incredible Journey*

*I enjoyed the experience this summer in China, and I know it is going to aid me in the establishment of my own ministry for the Lord. I do believe I planted seed for future Christians and was used of the Lord in some way with three decisions for Jesus Christ as Lord and Savior.*

*I plan to write another report in much more detail as soon as I arrive home.*

*Otis S. Goodwin*

# 6

## Paving a New Path

> For I know the thoughts that I think toward you, saith the Lord, thoughts of peace, and not of evil, to give you an expected end.
> 
> Jeremiah 29:11 KJV

**September 1, 1984**

Otis arrived home from his studies in China and hit the ground running. He was excited to know that the Lord had given him a far-reaching vision and plan for a ministry with the national leaders in the 10/40 missionary window. Working with the national workers in these countries appeared to be the way to reach these countries with the gospel. While it was all fresh in his mind, he sat down and drew up a proposal for our church and the mission organization that we were associated with at that time. The following is the "Outline of Proposal" that we presented to our home church and the mission board.

*Note: The following statistics are from the early 1980s, and in the future decades, they have become even more critical.*

I. Purpose of our ministry:

   A. To help evangelize the two-thirds of the world's population (more than 3.2 billion people) in the 10/40 window
   B. To establish within the United States a network of believers and churches to support prayerfully and financially the above described work
   C. To create an awareness in the free evangelical world of the needs of the thousands of unreached people groups
   D. To inform the churches that 85% of the people living in this window are the poorest of the world's poor
   E. To make known that Islam, Buddhism, and Hinduism are centered in this window
   F. To increase the 1.25% of mission giving going to work in this window

II. Method of our ministry:

   A. To start a program of travel to churches and organizations in order to encourage prayer and gain financial support.
   B. To discover and explore ways in which our ministry could effectively and quickly help evangelize the unreached.

III. Location of our ministry:

    A. Near mission agency
    B. Near diplomatic circle
    C. Center of country (East Coast)
    D. Near population center and the Bible Belt

Once this proposal was approved, we had to start implementing the ministry. The first item on our list was raising our support so we could work full time in ministry. This is called "deputation" or, as some call it, "prefield ministry." Deputation is the process of going to churches and raising your personal support. Little did we understand that this process would be ongoing as long as we lived. Otis continued to do this up until a few months before he died, and I have continued to go through this process of raising funds and reporting to churches on the ministry.

When you begin deputation, you always start with friends and local churches. Our first mission conference was in a little church in Jefferson, Maine. Our second conference was in Machias, Maine. It was at these first churches that we met faithful friends, prayer partners, and supporters who have continued up until the writing of this book. As we started this journey of raising our support and traveling, it became a "growing in faith" adventure.

This first trip was an experience I will never forget. As we began this new journey, we only had funds for the first part of our trip. We had a full tank of fuel, and that was it. We had no funds for food or coffee. Love offerings were saving us from going hungry and supplying fuel for our car. After the service at one church, a young couple came up to me with a small baby in their arms. You could tell they were of little means. They expressed how much they appreciated us coming and sharing, and the young man handed me a $5 bill. My first thought was to give it back, as I thought they probably needed it more than we did, but I didn't. I have never forgotten receiving that $5 bill. "Little is much when God is in it."

We spent the next seven months traveling all over New England raising financial and prayer support. It was an overwhelming time for us. The friends we made and times of fellowship in homes and churches made it a life-changing time for us. There is no way I can express how grateful I am for those early days and for the friends who have stood with us to this day. During this period, we were able, by God's grace, to raise 50 percent of our personal support.

We had finished our internship at Calvary Bible Baptist Church, and we were ready to move forward. Otis was convinced we should pack up and move back to Virginia to be close to our mission board headquarters in the middle of the eastern United States and close to international airports as well. That would put us living in northern Virginia, one of the most expensive areas in the country. Otis believed that the timing was right to move and trusted that God would provide and take of us. I had more reservations about the move, and I was realistic that it was going to be a challenge. At this time, we only had 50 percent of our support raised. Deep down I knew God had taken care of us all through college which was a bigger challenge than what was ahead of us now. Even though my faith was wavering, I did not raise any issues regarding the move.

Otis' sister, Marion, traveled with me to northern Virginia to find a place to live. We were able to rent a three-bedroom, two-level townhouse close to both Jana's school and the mission office. This was in Chantilly, Virginia, and this townhouse became our first office.

## Memories

The church gave us a going away party and Neota Grady, Otis and my eighth-grade teacher, came to the party. She shared this testimony with everyone:

*Just 30 years ago, on Halloween in 1953, at the Kings Mills school party – when Otis drew his fortune, this is what it said –*

> *Full of pep and a willing worker*
> *Is she who your lot will share;*
> *She'll be a little quick-tempered*
> *For she had red hair.*

*From the shout that went up from the rest of the pupils, I gained an inkling of a budding romance. They were both in the eighth grade.*

*Now a lapse in time until October 1958, when Otis and Roxann were married in Whitefield Union Church by the Rev. Martin Storms. When Otis came for me to pin on his boutonniere, he nearly got cold feet when he saw the full church. He said, "Awful crowd, isn't there?" In the meantime, the girls were in the entry along with Roxann's dad. While trying not to crush the pretty dresses, Ted got plaster dust on the shoulder of his black, swallow-tail suit. I followed him three or four pews as he started down the aisle, frantically rubbing off the plaster with a tissue.*

*After the reception, they left for their honeymoon only to appear back within minutes to get their marriage certificate. They were afraid the people where they stayed overnight wouldn't believe they were married.*

*Now after three lovely daughters, two fine sons-in-law, two lovely grandsons, several types of work over the years, they are at last happily involved in the Lord's service.*

*May the very best of everything follow them throughout the rest of their life together.*

*These are my thoughts for you, Roxann and Otis and your family.*

*Neota Grady*

On April 1, 1985, Otis, Jana, and I traveled back to Virginia and moved into our townhouse. Jana was in a Christian school, I worked in the mission office, and Otis worked in the home office, all the while calling pastors to book meetings. We continued to travel all over the eastern United States from Maine to Florida and everywhere east of the Mississippi. We had dear friends, Ed and Lily Hidalgo, who took care of Jana when we were gone and treated her like a daughter. This was a tremendous blessing for our family and especially for Jana.

We started implementing our mission plan and raising funds for the ministry. We were not only continuing to raise support for us personally, but now for Bibles and materials for these countries.

Money was tight, but God continued to meet our needs. Soon after we moved to Virginia, Jana needed to go to the dentist for a check-up. After her appointment the dentist came to me and said that she needed braces, and she needed them soon. I thought, "Oh my word, what in the world will we do?"

We found a directory of Christian professionals and businesses in the northern Virginia area, and a local orthodontist was listed. I called to make an appointment, and we went to the first visit knowing they charged $25 for the initial appointment. I waited in the waiting room while Jana was being checked.

Soon the orthodontist and Jana came out, and he said, "Jana and I have been discussing the situation. She needs braces."

I was in a state of shock and my question was, "When?"

He replied, "Yesterday."

My second question was, "How much?"

He said Jana told him we were in full-time ministry, and he said, "I tell you what I am going to do. I am going to put braces on Jana, and I will send you a bill. If God gives you the funds for her braces, you can pay me; if not I will do Jana's braces for free."

I was overwhelmed, and I told him that gave me goosebumps.

He said that those were "holy bumps."

We never did receive a bill.

In 1985, I went to China for my first overseas trip. We had a team of 10 people, and we were touring the country. We climbed the Great Wall and visited the Terracotta Army museum. We visited with dear friends in Harbin, China while we were there to see the famous ice and snow sculptures. What a blessing to visit with friends while we were in China for 10 days. During this trip we were carrying materials we had picked up in Hong Kong for friends that Otis had made on his previous trip. We had many supplies, and my suitcase was full. This was a new experience for me, and I didn't realize at the time, but I would have more opportunities to be carrying precious gifts on many trips and travels. I was very nervous and not sure if I was ready for this adventure. This was my first trip, and little did I realize this was just the beginning of me carrying materials not welcomed by the government and taking such a risk. We knew that we had a purpose and a goal for our ministry and taking risks like this would soon become part of my new life in ministry.

Little did we realize, in just a few short months, our world and ministry would be turned upside down again. In September 1986, Otis was called into the director's office. It was explained to him that the ministry we were involved with did not fit into their vision. They requested that he take the ministry and move on to another organization. To make matters more complicated, they wanted me to stay and work in their office.

So, what were we supposed to do now? We were raising funds for Bibles and supporting nationals in some of our targeted countries. We still needed to raise more funds for our personal support. We were at a complete door closing. I was devastated, crushed, and perplexed all at the same time.

> *Without counsel purposes are disappointed: but in the multitude of counsellors they are established.*
> Proverbs 15:22 KJV

We left the mission office and went immediately to see our pastor, Steve Reynolds, at Capital Baptist Church just outside the beltway in northern Virginia. Otis always believed in seeking counsel. At this point, we were totally lost as to what we were to do next. Otis decided he needed to go to Maine to seek counsel from our sending church, Calvary Bible Baptist Church. At this time the church was without a pastor. Otis went with a plan to go back to Maine to work as in interim pastor until the church found a new pastor and continue to work the ministry. He presented the plan to the deacons.

Mr. Ziegler, an elderly and wise man of God, listened to the plan. Then he said, "No, Otis. We are not going to let you do this. If you do this, you will not be able to do your mission work because you will be so caught up with church ministry that your mission work will fail."

Looking back, this was the beginning of a new mission ... a new plan. However, Otis came home without a clear view of the direction we should take.

In my despair, I did have sense enough to keep saying to Otis, "You need to call Dr. Bruckner." After a few days, Otis did call and talk with Dr. Bruckner, and he encouraged us to start a new mission organization.

So now the question ... how do you start a mission agency?

# *If God is in it ...*

> To preach the gospel in the regions beyond you, and not to boast in another man's line of things made ready to our hand.
>
> 2 Corinthians 10:16 KJV

**September 1986: A New Beginning**

After much time of prayer, seeking guidance, planning, and evaluating all the ideas that were put before us, we began to realize if we were going to move forward with the vision God had given us, we needed to start a new mission organization. We were convinced that God had called us to continue the work in the "regions beyond."

So here we were at a crossroad again. We were still living in a two-level, rented townhouse in Chantilly, Virginia. Jana was in a Christian high school with no discount on tuition, and we were still only receiving half our monthly support. So, the BIG question was … how do you start a mission organization?

We knew we needed prayer and financial support, a name, a board of directors, a location, accounting procedures, a vision statement, a budget, office equipment, a checking account, funds, legal advice, and much more that we didn't even know about at the time. We were working to complete many projects at the same time in order to send out a letter to our supporters in hopes to start receiving prayer and financial support. We wanted our supporters to see much progress had been made in a very short period of time.

We hit the ground running. We had a network of friends and pastors who were helping us move forward and giving us support and counsel. As was our normal lifestyle, we didn't have any funds to start a new organization. Otis called his mother, and she gave us $500. A close friend gave us $250. So, we had $750 to start our organization.

I had worked in the financial office of the previous organization under a very dear friend, Jerry Knisley. (Years later, Jerry's wife, Mary, came to work with us and proved to be a great asset to our organization.) This experience working with Jerry proved to be valuable, as I knew what was needed for our financial process. We had enough funds to order the old one-write system of bookkeeping. One major requirement was to begin the process for our nonprofit, tax-exempt, 501 C-3 status with the Internal Revenue Service and the Commonwealth of Virginia. This needed to be accomplished so that we would be allowed to give donors a tax-deductible receipt for their donations.

Otis was working on raising up a board of directors. These faithful men of God stood with us for many years to come. The Lord was helping us build a team for the future ministry.

We had absolutely nothing to set up for an office. As we moved forward it was an overwhelming experience, as well as a learning experience to see God provide. We prepared our little spare bedroom to become an office, taking down the bed and leaning it up against the wall. We began to collect the items we needed. We had a file cabinet given to us; a friend gave us a word processor and a table to put it on; and we had a second-hand copier given to us as well. Unfortunately, we didn't have room in our little office, so the copier went into the kitchen. Otis would often lay hands and pray over it just to keep it working! He would say, "The devil lives in copiers," but it served us well for many years. One of our board members took me to an office supply store and bought file folders and paper to stock up our supplies. Otis used a lawn chair for his office chair, and thankfully we already had a desk. There was room for only one person to work in the office at a time!

One item we still needed was a typewriter. The one we had belonged to Julie when she was in high school. It was a cheap typewriter, and many of the keys didn't work. One morning Otis mentioned to me that there was an office supply company in Chantilly. He decided he was going to go and ask the owner if he would donate a secondhand electric typewriter to the ministry.

After we prayed Otis went to the store and was told that the gentleman was busy and unavailable. After a while Otis went back and was told he was not in that day.

A few days later Otis decided he would go one more time, and if he wasn't successful, he wouldn't return. After we prayed Otis left and was gone for quite some time. I was downstairs doing laundry when Otis came in. He sat down on the stairs and said, "You aren't going to believe this," and started to tell me the story.

The owner met Otis when he arrived at the store and invited him into his office. Otis explained to him that we were starting a new mission organization working with unreached people in Southeast Asia. Otis explained that we were located just down the street from the company and that we needed a typewriter; just a secondhand one would be sufficient. The gentleman looked at Otis and said, "Otis, what was the Lamb?"

Otis replied, "Jesus."

Again, he asked Otis, "What was the Lamb?"

By this time Otis was thinking, *"Lord, you are trying to teach me something."* Otis replied, "The Sacrifice or Savior."

After a few seconds, he said to Otis, "The Lamb was without spot or blemish. If I am going to give to the Lord, I can only give something that is without spot or blemish." He got up and went into the warehouse and came back with a box that contained a new Olivetti ET112 fully electronic typewriter and handed it to Otis.

What a lesson on God's provision and what an encouragement to us!

> But with the precious blood of Christ, as of a Lamb without blemish and without spot.
>
> 1 Peter 1:19 KJV

Another major decision that needed to be made was a name for our new organization. This took much prayer, discussion, and input from many friends. We knew we would be working in Southeast Asia, and we knew we would be working with the national Christian workers. We also had to make sure we didn't duplicate another organization's name.

Finally, Outreach To Asia Nationals (OTAN) was the name chosen! The foundation and goal was to reach the national believers so that they could reach their own people – "Nationals Reaching Nationals."

In September of 1986, we sent our first prayer letter from our home and new office to inform our church and friends of the new beginning. We had been busy, and God had blessed. In October 1986, we had our first organized board of director's board meeting. At this time, we were supporting seven national pastors. Over the next two years Otis and I traveled over 50,000 miles from north to south and east to west all over the United States. We were able to gain more visibility for the ministry in churches which resulted in an increase of partnership and support. This provided traction for the ministry in prayer and financial support. The support for nationals was increasing as well as the funding for Bibles, and we were able to send more Bibles and materials into these countries.

Once we got everything organized and moving forward with our new ministry, Otis made another trip to China. This trip was to connect with pastors in new areas of the country. During this trip Otis became very ill, and it took several weeks for him to recuperate. It took some time for the doctors to determine what was causing the illness, and infectious disease doctors were called in. They wanted to know where Otis had traveled. During his time abroad, he had traveled to inner Mongolia, and clean food was scarce. Eventually, they were able to determine the cause. He was diagnosed with brucellosis, a bacterial infection from eating infected lamb. He would have periodic attacks such as feeling fine at night, but then he'd wake up with a high fever, chills, aches and pain, and totally drained of energy. Each episode would last a week or so. They eventually lessened and finally stopped completely.

As we were moving forward, we started "The Labor of Love" project to raise money to put Chinese Bibles in the hands of house church believers. We began this endeavor in the spring of 1989, and Otis chose this name because he was asking churches to take a one-time offering on Labor Day Sunday. I can remember seeing him sit at our kitchen table calling pastors (we didn't have a telephone in our little office). He was so excited because most of the pastors he called agreed to take up an offering. The table was covered with telephone books, as he was a collector of telephone books! Everywhere we went, we gathered up telephone books from that area of the country. Most churches very seldom change their telephone number, and he used the telephone books to find churches to contact. This project was very successful.

After a few years we designated a portion of these funds for training pastors and Christian workers. Many years prior, during the Cultural Revolution in China, all the Bible schools were closed. As a result, the pastors that Otis met all desired and requested training. To this day, training national pastors to teach and train their own people and giving them the tools they need is a major priority for OTAN. As Otis began to travel more in these countries, he realized there was such a tremendous need for God's Word. Many churches had only one Bible. They would tear out portions of the Bible and share it with one another in their congregations or village. The need is still great to this day.

The ministries were all moving forward, but we were about to experience a difficult challenge in our family. Otis and I had been to a meeting, and when we returned home there was a message on our answering machine from our daughter, Julie. They were on their way to a medical center in Maine with Michael, our 4-year-old grandson. Michael had been sick, and when they took him to the doctor, they were told that his condition could be sickle cell anemia, systemic bacterial infection, or leukemia. The initial blood work did not show any of these illnesses. After a bone marrow test, it clearly showed Michael had Acute Lymphoblastic Leukemia (ALL). A blessing in all of this, however, was that the doctors felt he had only had leukemia for about 30 days. We claimed the following verse:

> And we know that all things work together for good to them that love God, to them who are called according to His purpose.
> Romans 8:28 KJV

Our family loved God and knew God would work all things for the good of our lives and in Michael's life. The next weeks were days of much prayer, trusting God, inner suffering for Michael, and comforting for Michael and his parents. He began a challenging two-year period with chemotherapy, and he went into remission very quickly. The doctors gave him a 90 percent chance of full recovery. Michael's brother, Andrew, was only a few months old when Michael was diagnosed. Michael was in and out of the hospital. It took our whole family to care for both Michael and Andrew. Michael came off treatment for a year and a half, but then had to go back on treatment with chemotherapy and cranial radiation for another year. After those challenging years of treatment, he continues to be cancer free to this day. Praise God!

I still had office work to keep up to date, plus we were back and forth to Maine helping to care for our family. Jana was in high school and had just returned from her first mission trip to Australia. We had scheduled meetings in Florida for two weeks, and Otis was preparing for a month-long trip to China, Laos, and Vietnam. God knew what our schedules were and what we needed to accomplish, and He gave us the strength and guidance to get through this very difficult time in our lives.

In the spring of 1989, we had outgrown our little rented townhouse in Chantilly, Virginia, so we started searching for a larger one to rent. We moved to Centreville, Virginia, renting a three-level townhouse which had a full basement for our office. Jana was in her senior year of high school, and we were traveling and raising funds for national support and Bible projects.

Our personal support was increasing, the ministry was growing, and we were receiving good responses from churches even though our ministry concept was new among American churches. In October we took a trip to California. Otis wanted to show me the high school in San Diego where he graduated from. After touring the area, we took a train up to San Francisco. This was just days before the big San Francisco earthquake of 1989. We had made plans to visit with David Yu, Moses Yu's son. Moses was the author of the Yu Study Bible, which was the first Bible we raised funds for to put Bibles into the hands of national pastors. Moses was in

China at this time, so we were not able to meet him. What a privilege to meet David and to listen to the history and the story of the writing of this study Bible. Later, Moses came to visit us and was able to be part of our board meeting by sharing his story. It was an honor to meet this man of God who had such a vital part of our ministry. Moses spent 20 years laboring to produce a study Bible to meet the needs of the persecuted saints in China.

In January 1990, we received a letter from the investment company we were renting from with the notice that they were selling the townhouse. So here we were at another crossroad in our ministry. We were informed that we could rent on a month-to-month basis. We had to focus on finding a place to live that functioned as living quarters and an office facility. We were living in the most expensive county in America. At this point our board decided we should purchase property and settle down. We knew we had to move to an area that was not so expensive, but we still needed to be close to an international airport.

Otis and I began a five to six-month search. We went west and south of Fairfax County, day in and day out. It was rather difficult to look at buying a piece of property without funds for a down payment and nothing to sell. We started searching for property on the route 81 corridor in the Shenandoah Valley of Virginia. We found a place and contacted the realtor to set an appointment to view the property. It wasn't ideal, but we figured we could make it work for a few years and build on an addition for the office. We were getting desperate. We made an appointment with a local banker to see what could be done for financing as the property was in foreclosure. Well, it didn't take long for the banker to make his decision. He said, "I know you people live by faith, but the bank doesn't live by faith." That door was closed.

We drove to Winchester, Virginia, stopped at a laundromat, and picked up a book with houses for sale and rent. We searched through the book and came across an ad which read, "A house for sale, owner financing, make an offer." Wow! This is just what we needed. We contacted the realtor, and she took us immediately to see the property. It was four miles west of Route 81 and about a half mile off the main highway. The road was like a snake's back. It was washed out in many places and very steep with a 90-degree curve halfway up, almost to the point of being impassable. There was only one neighboring house at the beginning of the road, and because it was the middle of June, the trees were all budded out and hiding the neighbor. We finally reached the end and came up to a beautiful house with a big detached garage, plus a small two-story barn with deck. The lawn was mowed so it looked nice, and we were told that the house was empty. The first thing I noticed when I entered the house was a big kitchen with beautiful cherry cabinets and a large living room and dining room with a wood stove. It was a split-level house with three bedrooms and two full baths upstairs. The downstairs basement was mostly finished with an outdoor entrance, a wood furnace room, and a laundry room. It also had heat pumps for electric heat if needed. The basement would be perfect, with little renovations, for an office. It was on three acres of land, and it was ready for immediate occupancy. We were beside ourselves with possibilities for our home and the OTAN office. The detached garage was very large, and we could picture how easily it could be renovated for a future office.

We were excited as we talked with the realtor and learned that the seller had just bought a place to live, and this property's sale had fallen through the same day they purchased their new property. We arranged to meet with the sellers the following day, and we stayed in Winchester that night touring around the city. Jana would be in college in the fall so this would be convenient for our family.

We met with the owners and learned that they were Christians. The price of the property was $120,000, and they were willing to carry the mortgage. There would be a three-year balloon payment. The interest rates were a little high, but we knew beyond a shadow of a doubt this was the place the Lord had provided for us. After searching for a place to live for many months, we moved on July 4, 1990 into our new home and OTAN office. A couple years later we were able to get a loan from the bank to pay off the sellers. It was a miracle that this was accomplished in a short period of time. We quickly updated and decorated the basement for our new office, and we were in business.

We were moving forward, the ministry was growing, and we were supporting more pastors and sending more materials into the "Regions Beyond." A year after we moved to Winchester, we were reporting on OTAN's ministry at Reston Bible Church and shared our vision for the garage to be renovated into an office. A member of Reston came forward and said he would be willing to take on the responsibility of this project. Along with this church and other supporting churches and individuals, funds were raised to renovate the garage into an office.

There were two additions to the garage which resulted in five offices, a conference room, a bath with a shower, a kitchenette, and a reception area. In April 1992, we planned a dedication service. Not quite as fast as Nehemiah built his wall, but close. What a miracle! We were moving to our fourth office facility and each time it was getting better and better.

Otis and several team members were traveling to several different countries. When not traveling overseas, we were on the road visiting churches across the United States. We were raising funds to support nationals, the Study Bible Project, and the Labor of Love Believer's Project. God was blessing. We were receiving reports frequently of people from the underground churches coming to know the Lord.

All of this was not without obstacles. Otis and a team were preparing to go to Vietnam for pastoral training, but the trip was about to be challenged. Otis began to experience another difficult health problem. I had to rush him to Winchester Medical Center one night with severe abdominal pain. He was rushed into surgery with a bowel obstruction due to adhesions from his ileostomy years earlier. He was in the hospital for a month and then endured several weeks of recuperation. God, in His infinite mercy and grace, allowed this to take place before he was on his way to Vietnam and not while he was there. The team went on to Vietnam and the training was successful. What a blessing to know that even when Otis was not able to travel, the team went on and had a productive training with our Vietnamese pastors. Otis always said, "If this is Otis and Roxann's ministry it will fail; if it is God's ministry it will move forward."

We were moving forward. We had staff coming on board, volunteers traveling overseas, and several pastors from across the United States traveling overseas to train nationals in each of our targeted countries. The first years of the ministry, Otis and I did not travel together too often. I had traveled with other ladies into these various countries for women's training. In the fall of 1994, Otis was preparing to travel to Vietnam and Cambodia. He wanted me to meet him in Bangkok, Thailand following the training in Vietnam and travel with him into Cambodia. Security was tight in both of these countries. A couple of American pastors and Otis were training pastors in Vietnam when they had a difficult experience. (You can read about this experience in the testimony titled "Hiding Under the Table" at the end of this chapter.) After the training in Vietnam was completed, we would be going into Cambodia. I was preparing to fly to Bangkok to meet up with Otis along with the others traveling with us. Just before I left home, Otis called me from Bangkok to tell me of the current political situation in Cambodia. The Khmer Rouge, a communist terror group, had run rampant killing over a million Cambodian people over several years. Otis was informed that this terror group was kidnapping foreigners and had just captured a group of Germans traveling on a train. This was what Otis called to tell me the night before I was to fly to Bangkok! We met in

Bangkok and prayed concerning our travel into Cambodia. Otis was convinced that the Lord would have us travel to there, so we went.

**Serving in Cambodia**

It was a short flight from Bangkok into Phnom Penh, the capital of Cambodia. As we were preparing to land, Otis alerted our team to pray that we would get through immigration quickly and with no issues. I was getting more nervous by the minute. Finally, I said to Otis, "Are you sure this is what the Lord would have us to do? It is one thing for you to get kidnapped but for both of us to get kidnapped and killed wouldn't help our family or the ministry." I realize now that it was a little late to ask this question. Otis looked at me and said very sternly, "Roxann, we have to serve God; we cannot serve fear."

So, with fear and trembling I got up from my seat and walked out onto a very dark landing field. It was quite a distance from the terminal. There were police everywhere with AK-47 rifles ready and willing to spring into action for any situation that might arise. I went up to the counter and handed my passport to the attendant, and she started asking me questions. Of course, I didn't understand what she was saying. We had a Vietnamese traveling with us as our translator. He translated to me that I didn't have any blank pages in my passport, and that I needed to pay $10, so they could stamp over another country's stamp. I gladly paid the $10.

After we registered, things went smoothly from that point forward. Our host took Otis and me up to our room. We unpacked, and Otis was sitting on the bed watching CNN. I was propped up on the bed cross-stitching when all of a sudden, Otis jumped up and started hitting the wall at a very big rat! (Really … a big one!) Needless to say, the rat was faster than Otis. Otis called down to the lobby and told them we had a rat in our room. Shortly after, a young lady came up to our room and was bedside herself laughing.

She said they usually leave when someone comes into the room! To me it was not a laughing matter. I told Otis I was going down to the lobby to sleep; it was better to be in the lobby with all the police bearing guns than to stay in a room with a rat. They decided to move us to a different room.

The next morning, we traveled to a village outside of Phnom Penh where there were 48 pastors waiting to be trained in the Word of God and learn practical application of the Word for everyday living. These pastors had nothing in the way of spiritual tools except a willing heart and a determination that even Satan fears. One elderly pastor had a pencil that he was taking notes with, and it was so short that he was holding on to the metal portion that holds the eraser. However, he never missed a word spoken. These men sat on plank benches and the floor for two full days to hear the Word of God.

We had collected eye glasses to give to the pastors and their families. What a sight to see as these precious people tried on glasses and were filled with joy when they could see. There was also sadness when the glasses weren't the right fit.

They served us fish for lunch, and it was good. Later, we were walking along the river, and we could see the people bathing and washing clothes in the river. I then realized I had just eaten fish that had come out of that river! By God's grace I did not get sick.

With the training completed, we were on our way back to the hotel. As we were coming into the city of Phnom Penh going around a rotary, our van was stopped by five police officers with guns. Otis was in the passenger front seat. Our driver was carrying on quite a conversation with one of the police officers while the others were walking around the van. After a while Otis asked the driver what they wanted. He said, "They want coffee money." Otis reached in his pocket and gave the officer a $5 bill. They took the money and scattered. We discussed this later and wondered if it was considered a bribe. Otis said it was the cost of doing business! I really didn't care what it was called; I was just glad to get out of the situation we were in and not end up in the police station or kidnapped. The next morning, we prepared to fly back home.

I have had people ask me if there were times when I was frightened in all those years while traveling. I reply, for the most part, no. But I admit that I was more frightened by the rat in our room than I was by the guns!

After this trip, I wasn't sure if I was ready to travel again but even though this was a challenging trip in many ways, I continued to travel to the "Regions Beyond" for many years. I did return to Cambodia in 1998, as well as in 2009 for women's training.

Along with traveling overseas, we were busy with local travel raising support for the nationals, materials, Bibles, and prayer support. We were involved in promoting missions in local churches that did not have an organized mission's program. We committed to a three-year program with these local churches, and it proved to be very successful. As I mentioned before, Otis collected telephone books everywhere we traveled, and they were a great source for finding local churches. We would go into an area and stay for a few days, and we would purchase a map (no GPS in those days) and map out a travel schedule to visit churches cold turkey. We had a very successful way of building up a speaking schedule for months ahead to present the OTAN ministry, as well as, promoting a program for a successful mission program. We were enjoying a full life serving the Lord here and overseas.

### Are You Ready for the Unexpected?

"For my thoughts are not your thoughts, neither are your ways my ways, saith the Lord. For as the heavens are higher than the earth, so are my ways higher than your ways, and my thoughts than your thoughts." Isaiah 55:8-9 KJV

I can remember it just like it was yesterday; the time my father, Otis Goodwin, sat me down for one of his "serious" conversations regarding our family's and our ministry's future. He used to call these times our "family council meetings." He explained that we were at a crossroad; that God was shutting one door of ministry, and we needed to pray intently about where God would lead us next. He outlined three different possibilities of where he thought God was leading us. Of those three, the last possibility and, in his mind, the least likely option, was birthing a brand-new mission board dedicated to reaching people for Christ in restricted access countries in ways that really hadn't been done before. I remember so clearly him saying to me, "I really don't think this is the path we are going to take." It was almost as if he was saying, "God surely doesn't want me to start a brand-new ministry."

You can imagine my surprise when just a short time later, he announced that he really felt as if God was guiding and directing him and my mother to start Outreach To Asia Nationals. He wasn't sure how it was all going to unfold but was confident that God was changing his heart and the direction of his path and plans.

That time of decision had a huge impact on my life and the lives of many people. For me, a valuable lesson was learned in listening to and obeying God's call for your life and ministry. I saw firsthand how my father really believed that he was going to head in one direction, however, God led in a completely different and unexpected direction. I also witnessed his unwavering obedience to God's call once His plan was revealed.

As I reflect on what the Lord has done over the past 25 years and the impact that this ministry has had on so many different lives, I am amazed. My mind goes back to that pivotal time of decision. What if? What if he hadn't had the faith to step out and start down an unexpected path? Thankfully, we don't have to ask ourselves those questions.

God has truly blessed over the past 25 years, and the impact and fruit from one step of faith will only be fully seen and comprehended in eternity. God tells us, "my ways are not your ways … my ways are higher than your ways." My father learned that the unexpected was what was expected of him.

Jana Goodwin Moritz<br>
Fall 2011

## The Random Phone Call that Sparked Intrigue

My first contact with Otis Goodwin was in the early 1990s through a phone call. Otis was doing what most missionaries do – making phone calls to find opportunities to present his ministry to churches. Otis was old school; he would diligently make random phone calls to random pastors he had never met, trying to set up preaching engagements to present his relatively new ministry, Outreach To Asia Nationals. As a pastor I received many calls from missionaries trying to find churches in which they could present their ministry. Unfortunately, most of the time I had to reject those missionaries because of scheduling issues or other reasons. Otis' phone call, however, was different than all the others. I am not sure why – was it his winsome personality, his ability to persuade, his heartfelt passion for the Lord and ministry? The longer I talked with him on the phone, the more I found myself unable to resist. I invited Otis and his wife Roxann to come present his ministry to Grace Baptist Church in Mt. Carmel, Pennsylvania. Little did I realize that phone call would be life-changing and would eventually take me around the world!

When Otis and Roxann came to Grace Baptist, it was obvious to all that they had a strong passion for the Lord and the ministry to which God had called them. Both of them went out of their way to make a personal connection with people. Before they left they actually offered to come again and do our Vacation Bible School or help us do an actual mission's conference, something we had never done before. Considering we were only a church of about 50 people at the time, his willingness to become involved with our little church made a major impression on me. Here was an executive director of a mission board who was willing to come to a church in the middle of nowhere to serve us. As they drove out of the parking lot, I felt that this was the beginning of a lasting relationship. Shortly thereafter, I invited Otis to come help us develop our mission's program.

At the time our church really needed help with missions. We virtually had no program. Before Otis came, we were giving about $350 a year to missions. We had a lot to learn. Otis drove up from Winchester, Virginia, and sat down with our people for several hours, teaching us how to have a mission's conference. In the end, Otis suggested we start with a three-year theme – Until the Whole World Sees, Until the Whole World Hears, Until the Whole World Knows. For the next three consecutive years Otis returned and preached our conferences using those three themes. The difference this made in our little church's giving was astounding. We went from giving $350 a year to $10,000 a year to missions with an increase in the general offering as well. In the end, the people of our church had a true heart for the mission field, and we were supporting 10 missionaries for $1,000 per year.

I can honestly say that just about everything I know about missions came through Otis Goodwin, yet at first his idea of training nationals seemed radical to me. I had never heard it before. Nevertheless, the more he talked about it, the more convinced I became that it was the best and most cost-effective method to reach the unreached. I have become such a proponent of training nationals to reach nationals that most of our missionary support to this day goes to national pastors. Since those early days I have been privileged to travel to several foreign fields including Guyana, India, and China, and those trips only reinforced my belief in the mission of OTAN.

Shortly after doing the three-year mission's program at my first church in Mt. Carmel, Otis invited me to come to a board meeting for OTAN in Winchester, Virginia. Then, in 1995 I was deeply humbled when he officially asked me to be a member of the board. It has been my privilege and honor to serve on the board of OTAN for the past 22 years. Recently I have taken on a new role with OTAN as the ministry manager for Vietnam. I will be taking yearly trips to Vietnam, working hands-on with the national pastors in assisting with training their own people. It brings great joy to my heart for my wife and I to work together on the mission field in Vietnam. God works in wondrous ways, and all of this started with that random phone call!

My fondest memory of Otis came one afternoon at Grace Baptist Church in Mt. Carmel. Both Otis and I were making preparations for that first missions conference. One of the men of our church had made a nice fundraising "thermometer" to show the progress of the giving commitments. But the thermometer needed a ribbon. Otis and I hopped in his van and went to the nearest store in town. It didn't take us long to find a ribbon that was suitable. I took the ribbon to the cashier to pay for it. That's when we encountered a problem. The cashier said, "That will be $1.63." Would you believe neither Otis nor I had $1.63 between us?! Otis said, "Wait, I think I have change in my van." As he went out to his van something unusual happened in the store. I was just standing in the store minding my own business, waiting for Otis to return, when a little boy ran quickly past me and accidently knocked over a mannequin. Scared, the little boy took off running. I thought I would be helpful and attempt to pick up the mannequin. I got down on the floor, put the mannequin's wig back on, put my arm around its waist and started to pick it up. About that time Otis came walking back in the store. Perfect timing! Otis looked at me and smiled and said, "What are you doing?!" We both laughed about it and went on.

That night when he preached, he told the church what had happened in the store that afternoon. Only Otis Goodwin could tell a story like this. It was quite embellished! He was very detailed as he told the church how shocked he was to return to the store only to find me, their pastor, on the floor hugging and kissing this blonde in the store! Everyone in the church was on the edge of their seats in a hushed silence! He told the story so convincingly I was wondering if they would ever believe the truth. When he finally broke out laughing and told them the true story, I was greatly relieved. Otis was one of the sincerest men I have ever met, but I always enjoyed his good humor and ability to make people laugh.

I will be forever grateful for Otis' friendship and influence on my life. Thank you, Otis and Roxann, for making a huge investment in our lives.

Pastor Jim

### Catch the Excitement

There are only a few people in my life who have deeply marked me for good. Otis Goodwin is one. My memories of Otis are all wonderful ones. He was always an encouragement to me. I can still clearly see his face, bright eyes, smile, warm words, and great faith. My life has been affected greatly and forever changed. Each memory puts a little joy in my heart, a smile on my face, and even a laugh of sheer fun.

The first time I met Otis it felt like he was a longtime friend. He made me feel like I was the only one that mattered. God used him to impact me and the churches I pastored for missions. He invited me onto the OTAN board, where I have served now for over 20 years. He caught me up in his passion for Asia, bringing me to China with him and encouraging me to go to Nepal on another occasion. He was the one who God used to fulfill my call to pastor in New England. He facilitated my coming to pastor Calvary Bible Baptist Church in Whitefield, Maine, his home and sending church, in 1998.

I miss him. I have no one in my life like him. May God raise up more who will share his passion for Jesus, his love for people, and his faith to trust God for big things all for God's glory.

Jerry Wright<br>
Our Pastor and Friend

## Hiding Under the Table

In recent years Vietnam has made significant progress in religious freedom, but this was not the case after the war. Twenty years ago, apart from the registered government churches, the majority of Christians met in unregistered house churches.

Much of their worship had to be done in secret. If they had a Bible, it would be hidden in a paper bag or newspaper as they approached the house. They would arrive for services one at a time and leave one at a time. The secret police would often interrupt the Bible studies and worship services, arrest the pastor, and scatter the flock.

Much of the persecution was in the form of harassment. The pastor would be arrested, sentenced to a few weeks jail term, and then released and warned not to have any more church meetings in his house. Like the early church, these pastors had to obey God rather than man. They would immediately have worship again the following Sunday. After a few weeks, the secret police would break up the service, and the cycle was repeated.

These pastors had little or no training and even fewer resources. Most would have only a New Testament. Some may have a complete Bible. Rarely would a pastor have a Bible dictionary, concordance, or other Bible study help.

God gave Otis Goodwin, founder and director of Outreach To Asia Nationals, a heart and passion to train these pastors. Otis organized a curriculum and challenged North American pastors and teachers to teach the one-week sessions. It was my privilege to teach several of those early classes.

In one of those early classes, I was teaching about 25 pastors. Otis and another teacher were seated with the pastors. Suddenly the lookout came running into the room and anxiously spoke to the interpreter who immediately commanded Otis, the other teacher, and me to, "Get under that table right away!" We did exactly what he said, cramping ourselves into the corner under the table with our knees up to our chins.

The pastors began piling carpets, boards, and trash on top and around the table. Instantaneously the pastors left, and children were brought into the room. A Vietnamese woman wrote phrases on the blackboard in English such as: "Hello. How are you?" and "I'm fine. How are you?" The teacher would say the phrase and the children would repeat the phrase after her in unison. Apparently, someone had reported hearing English being spoken. When the secret police saw the English class, they departed without any further investigation.

What was unnerving to us was a common experience to these pastors. We relocated and continued sharing God's Word with these eager pastors. God gave each of us new insights as to the plight of the persecuted church.

Dr. JK<br>
Pastor

## Ministry in the Unexpected

In 1995, after 30 years working in various locations for a telephone company (Bell System), I was preparing to take an early retirement.

I received a call from a friend and fellow church member who was working with a missionary organization named Outreach To Asia Nationals. He told me they had a headquarters building, but only had a telephone at each end of the building. With the staff increasing in number, he asked if I could possibly get them a business telephone system to meet their needs. This was a very unusual request, but I told him I would see what might be available. After several calls I found a company that was upgrading their current telephone system and willing to donate their old system. It was the perfect size with an adequate number of telephones to meet the need for OTAN.

On a Friday in October of 1995, I traveled to the OTAN office in Winchester, Virginia to begin installing the system. Upon arriving I discovered the current building wiring was totally inadequate for the new system making it necessary to re-cable the entire building. This was not a one-man job, nor was it a quick installation. After discussing the situation with Otis Goodwin, director of OTAN, he suggested he could help me, and we could get the job completed together. So, we did. We worked late into the next morning with Otis crawling around in the attic pulling cables to where I needed them, allowing me to install the overall system.

At breakfast on Saturday morning, Otis Goodwin challenged me to seek the Lord regarding the services I could offer to missionaries and churches that had critical communication needs but could not acquire or afford them. He encouraged me to sincerely use these talents for the Lord by building a "mission" organization to accomplish the need.

Little did I know that Otis' encouragement and suggestions would lead to 18 years of serving missionaries and churches not only in the United States but overseas as well. What started as one man, with a vision from Otis Goodwin, has grown into a team of over 12 men and women consistently serving, with additional volunteers joining our team for larger projects. With the Lord's leading, countless organizations' communication needs have been met at virtually no cost to them for the equipment and no cost at all for the labor we were able to provide.

I had the pleasure and blessing of working with Otis on many other occasions. Thank God for a man dedicated to hearing the Lord's leading, even in support areas, to further the cause of the gospel throughout the world.

Dick Sand<br>Lynchburg, Virginia

## Faithfully Serving Behind the Scene

In July 1995, I received a newsletter from Otis and Roxann asking friends and donors to pray for a secretary/receptionist to join the OTAN team. I stood in my kitchen looking out the window and told the Lord, "I could do that! But, Lord, you will have to sell my house and help me get there." I started what I called my "Abrahamic journey" not knowing how, when, or where but willing to go help Otis and Roxann.

In April 1996, I was approved by the board and began planning my journey from southern Virginia back to northern Virginia and the new Winchester office. Otis and Roxann were most helpful to me while raising support and looking for a home in an area I was not familiar with at all.

God was good to give me the opportunity to go overseas on a medical team to Cambodia. Going to Cambodia was a life-changing event for me. I grew up poor in the hills of West Virginia. Cambodia's poverty was worse than anything I had ever experienced in my life. When I saw men with no clothes and only cloths wrapped around them, I was in shock. I helped raise funding for children to be adopted. Out of the 40 children adopted with our support, eight were by my friends. The rice grass huts in Cambodia had no furniture. They slept on mats and only had the clothes on their bodies and maybe another outfit hanging on the line. They drank river water that was not fit to drink. It came straight from the same river where the animals bathed as well as where the children bathed. There was one cistern for the entire village with one cup for all to share. Cooking was done over a hole in the ground.

Our Cambodian ministry manager said I had to go to the "killing fields" to fully grasp all the Cambodians had gone through. As I walked those grounds and saw all the skulls and torture rooms, I knew this was a horror story that needed to be told. I worked diligently to share it with as many as I could. My daily task was to count out vitamins for children. Some children had AIDS, and many had worms or other horrible ailments. We did all that we could do as we moved from village to village each day. One lady owned land and wanted to give it for a church to be built. Reston Bible built a church on that land. One village had a young teenager ministering to the little children. As we came into the village, they sang the praise song *Shout to the Lord*. It was such an awesome, inspiring event in my life.

I also had an opportunity to travel to Nepal with Roxann. Coming back home to OTAN was a blessing. I decided that overseas travel was not my calling. I just wanted to remain in the office doing all I could to keep things running smoothly and meet the needs of our staff and board. I loved working with Otis and Roxann Goodwin. I was blessed to have a 17-year part in the OTAN ministry!

Mary Knisley

**Additional notes from Roxann**

Mary was a blessing to the ministry and to our family. She was a great recruiter, and she recruited Dick and Judy Mihill who were faithful workers for many years in the office. What tremendous blessings this recruited couple was to the ministry and to our family.

My mom and dad's wedding announcement published January 25, 1933.

Otis' mom and dad's wedding picture. Old photographs are so neat!

Otis got to meet Wang Ming Da, founder of the house church movement in China. This man spent over 20 years in prison during the Chinese Cultural Revolution. Wang Ming Da is pictured here next to his wife.

Otis and me on our wedding day in 1958. We were so young and unaware of what God had planned.

This is the barn where we lived in North Whitefield, Maine during our internship after Otis graduated from Liberty University. That was one frigid winter!

Our first office in the townhouse was quite a sight! You can see the bed propped up against the wall and Otis' lawn chair that he used as his office chair.

Otis loved spending time with the children in Asia and giving them balloons, candy, or other little gifts.

Otis and I got to see the Great Wall of China. Otis would pass out tracts and share the gospel. You can see how happy the people were to hear.

Otis met Moses Yu and received a Moses Yu Study Bible from him. These Bibles helped national pastors in Asia learn and teach God's Word.

On my way to or from Bangkok, Thailand. We rarely traveled light since we often took supplies and teaching materials to the national pastors.

I got to ride an elephant in Bangkok, Thailand in 1994. We got to experience a lot of fun things when we traveled to Asia.

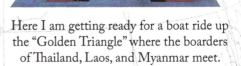

Here I am getting ready for a boat ride up the "Golden Triangle" where the boarders of Thailand, Laos, and Myanmar meet.

Training the national women was my main mission on my travels. In these three pictures from top to bottom you will see: Ladies in Nepal after hours of training. The ladies in China wearing fruits of the spirit crafts we made together so they could remember the lesson. Ladies in Vietnam making puppets to teach Bible lessons to the children. This was the trip to Vietnam where we had to hide during the police raid.

Otis often preached when he traveled. Here in Nepal, you will notice the men sitting on one side of the church while the women sat on the other.

Otis in Papua New Guinea when he received the birds-of-paradise.

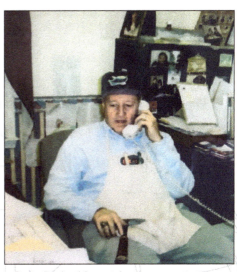

Before the road leading to the OTAN office and our house was repaired, it was often impassable after heavy snowfall in Virginia. We had to trek half a mile through the woods with our supplies. It was an adventure!

Otis, the builder, with a hammer in one hand and a phone in the other as he worked on the office addition.

The open house and dedication of the new OTAN offices was a joyous day. It is still the home of OTAN today.

Otis was so proud to welcome home our grandson, Corey, from a year-long tour in Iraq. Otis was determined to be there despite his health issues.

I simply want to share a handsome picture of Otis when he was healthy and dressed sharp.

My granddaughter Kristina and I traveled with a team to help at a Bridging The World Summer Camp in China in 2009. It was a rare experience for the people in that particular region to see Americans, and they wanted us to sing for them.

Here I am at a police station in Russia filling out a report after my shoulder bag was picked up by another passenger in the airport. All of my important papers to return home were in that bag. I received a phone call that night that it was returned to the U.S. Consulate. What a relief! I even kept the notes the police wrote about the incident.

I had the honor of giving this young man his first Bible in Russia. He was so happy.

Pastors in Nepal were so honored to receive Otis' shirts and ties after he passed away.

The OTAN office in Winchester, Virginia in summer.

The OTAN office in Winchester, Virginia in winter.

# Overcoming Hurdles

> But they that wait upon the Lord shall renew their strength; they shall mount up with wings as eagles; they shall run, and not be weary; and they shall walk, and not faint.
>
> Isaiah 40:31 KJV

In the late 1990s, the ministry was moving forward training pastors and Christian workers, and the women's ministry was beginning to become a major ministry with tremendous results. However, we were experiencing a greater hindrance from the governments, especially in Vietnam. Otis was making plans to go to Vietnam for training, and when I went to the Vietnam Embassy in Washington, D.C. to pick up his passport, I was told, "No visa."

This was quite a shock and very confusing for us. We did not receive any explanation for the refusal.

It took three years before he was able to receive a visa to enter the country again. In 1993, Otis met a special servant in Vietnam. She had worked for the U.S. government during the war, and she was not only a Christian, but she spoke English as well. She was the catalyst that God used to move the ministry in Vietnam to what it is today. She was a faithful servant and totally committed to OTAN for many years until her health was such that she passed the mantel on to the next generation. It was through this special contact that Otis was able to obtain a visa to go back into the country.

The ministry in Vietnam was fruitful; pastors were reporting that their churches were growing numerically as well as spiritually. At times the trainings had to be canceled due to government interruptions. We had two American pastors who were arrested, interrogated, fined, and sent out of the country. Even though Satan was roaring around trying to devour whom he could, the ministry was moving forward. The national pastors were determined that the gospel was going to move forward. When the training ministry started in Vietnam, all the curriculum had to be translated here in the U.S. and hand carried into the country. Also, funds for the support of pastors had to be hand carried into the country. There were not any wire transfers in those early days.

I was traveling to these different countries on a regular schedule training women. I had made plans to go to Vietnam even before the U.S. pastors were arrested. I kept my schedule, and so along with a friend, we flew to Vietnam. My friend was traveling with several hearing aids and batteries that were going to be given to an orphanage. Otis said she would probably be checked by security for the batteries, making her take them out and explain what they were for. As I mentioned, all the curriculum had to be hand carried into the country. Well guess who was the first person to go to Vietnam after the U.S. pastors were arrested? Me! I was carrying a full-blown curriculum for several trainings in my luggage. I knew I had many people praying for me to arrive safely and to have no problems through security with the curriculum. I went through security and started to put my luggage on the x-ray belt. There was a woman ahead of me, and when her bags went through, they stopped the moving belt, opened her bags, and started going through them. I was just standing there waiting when a man came up to me and said, "Give me your bags." He took my bags off the belt before they went through x-ray, and I grabbed my shoulder bag and followed him out to the sidewalk. My bags were right there, but when I looked up to see who had picked up my bags, he was gone. Not one person searched through my luggage before entering Vietnam. Do you believe in angels?

We were in Vietnam to train women, and one of our lessons was instructing the ladies on how to make puppets for teaching children. We were staying at a guest house, not a hotel. Once we arrived at the guest house, we stayed inside as it had a gated courtyard. The owner was a Christian, and she was planning to open a daycare. We were all sitting around with puppet material, Bibles, and curriculum everywhere when all of a sudden, the women jumped up and one lady took my friend and me up on the third floor. The police were at the gate. We were told to hide behind some cabinets. That way if the police should come into the room and just look, they could not see us. It seemed like an eternity, but soon they came to get us and told us all was clear.

When we went downstairs the women were all laughing and talking at once. The police questioned the owner as to why there were so many motorbikes in her courtyard. She told them that she was preparing to start a daycare, and she was getting ready. It was true that she was going to start a daycare. Once the police left, we were brought back downstairs. I looked around and there was not one Bible or piece of curriculum in sight. The women knew how to make things disappear in a hurry.

After the training that evening a couple of friends came and told us that they were going to take us out for the evening. It was around nine o'clock, and they came with motorbikes. So here I was an old grandmother riding on a motorbike through the streets of Ho Chi Minh City, holding on for dear life and wondering what in the world I was doing. We arrived at the water front, and there was a huge cruise liner with a band playing. We ventured on to the ship and listened for about an hour when the band started playing "Auld Lang Syne." We thought we were back in America on New Year's Eve.

In 1998, Otis was invited to go to Papua New Guinea with a missionary friend who had worked in New Guinea for many years. He would be speaking at a pastor's conference with several hundred pastors. It was during this time that Otis met some pastors who were willing to go to Vietnam to train other pastors. They were accepted by the Vietnamese government better than Americans, so these men were a great resource in training national pastors in Vietnam.

At the closing of the conference the leader said to Otis that they were going to give him a gift. With the American mindset, Otis thought the gift would be money, and he was trying to figure out how he could refuse the funds. The gift turned out to be two, not one but two, birds-of-paradise that had been stuffed and mounted. This was the national bird of Papua New Guinea. When our missionary friend saw this, he was overwhelmed and told Otis that he could not accept this gift let alone take them back to the United States. Otis decided he was going to pack them in his luggage and see what happened. The men were so pleased and excited when Otis opened the gift. This was very special. Otis left New Guinea and stopped in Australia to visit friends of ours. He bought two sheepskin rugs for me, and he had more trouble going through U.S. customs with the rugs than with the birds-of-paradise.

The ministry was moving forward. We had more staff; we had ministry managers for several of the countries; we were receiving encouraging news from our contacts in each of the countries, and we were receiving support from more churches. We were involved in supporting and building orphanages in Nepal, Russia, and Vietnam too. Otis decided we needed to move further in ministry. In 1999, we established Bridging The World ministry. OTAN was established to work in the restricted access countries of Southeast Asia. Bridging The World was for ministry anywhere else in the world.

What a blessing this ministry has been since it started. Capital Baptist Church sent out the first missionaries, Steve and Debbie Poston, who are also good friends of ours, to join BTW. They have served faithfully in this capacity in Mexico and started two churches and three mission plants. National pastors are now leading those churches. Several more churches have been planted from national pastors who studied at his Bible Institute as well.

Bridging The World's primary focus is sending full-time teachers to China as well as leading mission teams to teach conversational English to young children in summer camps. I took my granddaughter, Kristina, in 2009. My daughter, Jana, and granddaughter, Jaden, were part of the 2018 team. God has blessed this ministry through the years. Otis was always trying to recruit people for China. He never hesitated to say when he met someone, "I think that you need to go to China." One time he met a young woman at a conference, and when he mentioned this to her, she had already been praying about going to China. She ended up going with BTW and stayed for 10 years teaching English. What a blessing.

We were soon entering the early 2000 years. We had no idea what these years would have in store for us in ministry and in our personal lives. It was time to start preparing and planning for an addition to the office. But before we could begin the renovations, we first had to focus our attention on rebuilding the road going onto the property. The condition of the road was bad, and we had to start raising funds to begin the construction. We had plans drawn up, but we had to go to the county for permission. At first the county was giving us problems concerning the need for a turn lane from the highway into our road. The turn lane was going to be extremely expensive. After much prayer and meetings, they finally gave us permission to start the project without requiring the turn lane. Funds were starting to come in, and we were in business, or so we thought.

Otis decided to contact the person who owned the property on the right side of the road leading to the property to see if he would be willing to donate funds toward the new road, and we could give him a tax-deductible receipt. When Otis met with him, he told Otis that we did not have the right-of-way, and that he would not permit us to build the road unless we paid him a huge amount of money. Otis told him we had a deed stating we did have the right-of-way. To make a long story short, it was a big problem figuring out the legal issues with the deed, and it ended up being a big mess. After many months, we finally had a beautiful road that seemed like a boulevard to us. This was a major blessing from the Lord.

That very first day we went to see the property years ago, the agent told us there were 47 acres of land that bordered the property, and the only way to access the land was by using our road. Otis could envision OTAN owning that property for future use – a building for dormitories, apartments for traveling missionaries, and a training center. The owner of the property would periodically stop in just to say "hi." One day he told us he was putting the property up for sale. The land was laid out in 10 housing lots. After a time, Otis went to him and asked if we could purchase the property. The answer was no because he wanted to sell each lot separately. A couple of years went by with no purchaser.

After some time, Otis went to see the owner and asked if we could purchase the property, and again he replied, "No." We kept the property on our prayer list, and one day, the owner came and told Otis that the only people interested in the property was OTAN. We ended up purchasing the property for $47,000 for the 47 acres. The seller held the mortgage. We were to pay $7,000 per year for three years with no interest, and he claimed the would-be interest as a tax deduction. God was blessing, and after the third year God provided the money to pay off the loan. The owner said because of his tax situation he could not accept the balance. The next year he did, and we paid off the loan with a 10 percent deduction on the balance. Another major blessing from the Lord!

In 2001, we started the planning process of adding an addition to the existing building. We knew we needed office space to grow. We battled with the county for many months to obtain permits to build on to our existing building. Otis went to several meetings with the county supervisors, and there was even an article in the local newspaper. The article quoted one of the supervisors as saying he was concerned that terrorists might be trying to infiltrate the community under the disguise of a mission organization. Amid the frustration of this entire process, we couldn't help but laugh at this ridiculous accusation. Finally, the county did give us a conditional use permit. We had a very dear friend draw up the plans for the new addition. Once we received the permit, we were able to begin the construction on the addition.

The ministries were growing, and we added additional staff. Otis and I were traveling overseas on a regular basis, most of the time to two or three countries per trip. During our times of travel, we had some very interesting situations arise. Otis was on his way to board a flight from Washington Dulles to Bangkok, Thailand. He was carrying funds for pastor support and for his personal travel expenses. As soon as he was checked in and walking down the tunnel to board the plane, he was stopped by authorities and told that they needed to see all the funds that he was carrying. They made him lay out all his money on the floor while they counted all of it, including the foreign currency. People were walking by and observing this process. Otis was wondering what this was all about. Finally, after counting the funds, which came to a little less than $10,000, the authorities kindly explained to him that it was not illegal to carry more than $10,000 out of the country, but you were required to submit a form with the amount of money being carried. What a lesson!

Our family was growing, Kim and Randy had adopted two precious little girls, Kristina Marie and Jessica Marie. What joy they brought to our family. Jana and Gary Moritz were married just days after the September 11 terrorist attacks. He was in the Marine Corps, and we were not sure if he was even going to get time off to get married. Our five grandsons, Joshua, Lee, Corey, Michael and Andrew, were growing up fast, and Otis had the privilege of taking each one with him on one of his trips overseas.

In the summer of 2003, little did we realize that we were about to enter one of the most difficult times of our lives. We wondered if we were going to survive what we were about to face. Otis began to have severe painful gallbladder attacks that lasted for several weeks. Due to his previous surgeries, they decided they had to do major surgery. His pre-op tests were all good, and he went into surgery. Before they had him completely sedated, a heart problem showed up on the EKG, so the surgery was canceled. When he discovered that the surgery was canceled, needless to say he was not a happy camper. After the rain there is always sunshine. Jana and Gary soon announced they were expecting a baby in the spring. What a joy and excitement for our family. Otis was overjoyed. He relished being a grandfather, and I was glad that he was given this news before he had to go back for a second attempt at the surgery.

After several more tests he was once again cleared for gallbladder surgery. On October 8, he went in again for surgery, and after several hours the surgeon came to see me with unexpected news. They did remove the gallbladder, but the gallbladder was attached to the small bowel due to adhesions from his previous surgeries from ulcerated colitis when Otis was 28.

The surgeon told me there would likely be problems, and it would take about three days for the problems to show up. Sure enough, in three days the problems began. He had to go back into surgery on October 17 for an obstruction, and then back into surgery on October 20 for a leakage in the bowel. He was on a ventilator, his kidneys were starting to shut down, and he had to have dialysis and several units of blood. He remained unconscious and still on the ventilator until the middle of November. At one point they even had to shock his heart.

He slowly began breathing on his own, and they were slowly weaning him off the ventilator. One day, the doctor asked me if I thought they should try to wean him completely off the ventilator, and I said that we needed to try. By God's grace, he managed to breathe on his own – a major breakthrough! I had spent days talking to him, reading scripture, praying, and keeping him updated on our family even though I didn't know whether he heard me or not. There was no sign that he did, and he never remembered what went on during this time.

This was just the beginning of a very long and difficult time for us. First of all, it was close to Thanksgiving, and I had to deal with telling him all that had gone on the last several weeks and what the future held for us. The doctors did not give us any hope that he would fully recover physically, mentally, or emotionally. At this point Otis needed to realize that he had a long convalescence ahead. His bowels were still obstructed, therefore he could not have his incision closed. In other words, the ileostomy stopped functioning. The doctors would not give us a timeframe of when or if the incisions could ever be closed.

Otis was in Fairfax Hospital in Northern Virginia, which was an hour and a half away from our home in Winchester. His care was around the clock, and all his secretion came out of the open incision. I stayed with friends who lived almost next door to the hospital. He could not eat or drink, so he was on TPN and IVs daily for intravenous food supplement. I spent many hours in the hospital caring for him.

There was much discussion on how we were going to move forward. We knew this was going to be long term. The doctors decided Otis needed to go to rehab. Christmas was right around the corner, and everyone agreed he couldn't stay in the hospital long term. I decided to go see the rehab facility. I knew Otis would not be happy there and would not receive the care that he needed. God provided when the rehab facility refused to take him because he was too critical. I told the doctors that I would take him home and care for him. The doctors were hesitant, but finally agreed that we did not have a choice.

Now, we had to deal with the insurance company. When we moved to Winchester, we were grandfathered into the company that had covered our insurance for years. However, our home in Winchester was located out of their coverage area creating many inconveniences. By God's grace we managed. In order for the insurance to take care of us, we had to stay in northern Virginia. Jana and Gary lived in a townhouse in Leesburg. So we set up a hospital bed in their living room, and I slept on the couch. The home health nurse came in three times a week. Otis had to have weekly blood work to check levels and make sure the TPN was providing him with the proper nutrients he needed. He was on IV fluids every other day to keep him hydrated. Christmas came, and we were about to enter a new year and the unknown.

On one of the home health nurse visits, the nurse told us she lived near Winchester, and it would be very convenient for her to come to our home each visit. We were excited to hear that we might be able to move home. Soon she called us and said that the administration had agreed. So, we moved bag and baggage back home. What a blessing; after four months we were home. This did entail more inconveniences for Otis' care, but we were home. There is no place like home! We were only home for a short time when our insurance company changed their policy. The nurse was not allowed to come to our home, so that meant every week I had to take Otis into northern Virginia to get his labs taken, and then I had to go back to pick up his TPN for the week – seven bags each week. The TPN came in very large bags that I had to connect to his port, and it took 12 hours to complete the process every night. Over the next few months there were many crises, but we were home. He had two abdominal abscesses which were extremely painful, and he had to be admitted back into the hospital with high potassium. During this time our doctor was wonderful and gave me his mobile phone number with the instructions to call him anytime. I did call him a couple of times, and he was always very kind and helpful to us. One time he told me his goal was to keep one man alive!

> Thou wilt keep him in perfect peace, whose mind is stayed on thee: because he trusteth in thee. Trust ye in the Lord forever: for the Lord Jehovah is everlasting strength.
>
> Isaiah 26:3-4 KJV

Oh, how we were dependent on the Lord moment by moment to sustain us in this challenge on our journey of life. We were blessed to have a staff who kept the ministry moving. Otis would go to the office dragging his IV pole along, and he was involved in the day-by-day ministry. Other than going to the office and to the doctors, we were basically housebound. It was a challenge to go anywhere.

God was blessing our family. Jana went into labor with our new granddaughter. What a blessing for me to be in the delivery room when Jaden Noel was born. I will forever be grateful to Jana and Gary for letting me be involved in this special moment. Another blessing during this time that we were able to witness was our oldest grandson, Joshua Otis Bailey, graduating from Liberty University. No matter what the travel to Lynchburg involved for Otis, we were grateful for the ability to be present at this momentous time in his life.

In early April, we were told by our doctor that our previous surgeon would not be involved in the corrective surgery Otis needed. We were told they were transferring us to an outside colon/rectal specialist for the remainder of Otis' care. Otis was upset because we had built a great relationship with our doctor, but we knew we needed the best of care and this group of surgeons were well known for their expertise in this field. Our first visit did not go well. Otis asked the doctor when he could have the surgery to close his abdomen, and the new doctor would not give us a timeframe. He said it could be up to a year. This was devastating, and we were truly blown away by this news.

I do admit that it was difficult to have peace on our journey. We were very discouraged, and the surgeon was not encouraging. We were now into our seventh month, and we were told that it could be another year. Another potential problem was that Otis may not have enough bowel for reconstructive surgery. At the time of the original surgery in October, the doctor told me Otis had so many adhesions from previous surgeries that his bowels were like a cement block. I remember the day he went in for x-rays, and what a blessing and answer to prayer when the doctor informed us that Otis had plenty of bowel and there should not be a problem with the surgery.

There were financial hurdles during this time too. To prepare for surgery, I was going to have to give Otis weekly injections which I had done years before when he was suffering with the ulcerated colitis. The cost was $125 each week. There was no way we could afford this. I went back to our insurance company, and they reduced the cost to $25 per week. What a big blessing!

Finally, after two scheduled dates for surgery had been canceled, Otis went into surgery for the closing of his abdomen nine months after the original surgery. The surgery went well with no complications, and we waited for three days to see if his ileostomy would function. What a day of rejoicing it was when we were told it was functioning after so many challenging days, weeks, and months! It was only by God's grace that we survived and the prayers of people around the world that we came out of this difficult time.

Otis made plans the day he left the hospital to start packing his bags to go oversees again. Little did we realize that in three short years we would be facing more problems that would affect the ministry and our family for the rest of our lives.

## Write that Down

Otis and Roxann had a huge impact on our lives. One day in the late 1990s they stopped by our house to visit, and I was in our driveway changing the brakes on my car. The next thing I knew, Otis was there with his white shirt sleeves rolled up working right alongside of me. Actually, he took over, and we were able to complete the job in no time.

Christine and I had spent a year in China teaching English. We desired to spend the rest of our lives taking other Americans to the great land of China to teach English as well. I asked Otis if he would sit down and talk with me about our dream. Otis was such an encouraging person. He said in his Maine accent, "Yes! Right after church get two legal pads and pens, and we will sit down in the booth in the kitchen and plan this out."

So, I did as he said, and there we were sitting in that booth in the kitchen facing each other.

Otis began, "What do you want to do?"

I replied, "Take Americans to China!"

"Write that down," he directed. "What will you do when you get there?"

"Teach them English," I said.

"Write that down," he instructed again. "How will you get there?"

"We will fly," I replied.

"Write that down. How much will it cost?" he asked.

"I don't know," I said.

"Write that down," he continued. "Where will you stay?"

"At the school we taught at," I replied.

"Write that down …" was Otis' reply as the question-answer conversation continued for about half an hour until he finally said, "That's all! Now go do it!"

And so that was the beginning of the Bridging The World Summer English Camps for Christine and me in China! In 1997 I took three high school girls who were in my Chinese class on our first summer camp in China. Otis asked us to continue the summer camps that we started with his guidance, and we have not missed a year since. The ministry has grown, and we now average about 100 Americans teaching conversational English in the camps each year.

Otis and I stayed in contact with one another, and in January 2002 we met together in Hong Kong. I will never forget our first time together in China. Our first morning at our hotel, we were up early to meet together and talk. Otis asked me what we had been doing in China since 1995 when Christine and I came as teachers in a public high school in Beijing for the year. I told him about our experiences in bringing Americans to China to teach summer English camps for junior high and senior high Chinese students each year beginning in 1997, and Otis showed a lot of interest in the way we conducted summer camps. We continued talking for several hours, and then we headed out to meet a travel agent Otis knew and had used before to plan out our travels in China. First, he arranged for us to travel to Guangzhou by train, and then he had the agent arrange travel plans for us to visit each of my Chinese summer English camp contacts. Otis wanted to meet them all.

Our trip began with a visit to Samuel Lamb in Guangzhou. Pastor Lamb was persecuted for his faith by the Chinese government and imprisoned many years. When we went to see him, he met with us and was very cordial and responsive to our questions. We had prayer together, and it was apparent that he knew Otis and was pleased by our visit with him. Pastor Lamb died 10 years later in 2012. I am so happy I had the chance to meet him with Otis. After our time with Pastor Lamb, we met with one of Otis' key contacts in China. Our time with this man was interesting as he seemed to have a lot of contacts.

Once we settled into our hotel, we met with a Chinese friend whom he had met on his previous trips. Otis was so happy to see him. Otis had tears in his eyes, and right there I saw a passion for the Chinese people that I knew was from God! I translated for Otis as he asked many questions about this man's family and work and listened carefully in return to his replies. After this friend left the hotel room, Otis immediately went to his bed, got on his knees, and began crying like a baby! Then we prayed together which was truly heartfelt and showed Otis' love for the Chinese people as he prayed for this friend and his family and work in China. I never experienced prayer with anyone as I did with Otis that day in that hotel room. Otis' prayer flowed forth as if this was something he had been doing every day for years. Tears flowed, and I knew he had a relationship with God that was very, very special! I began to see God moving in my heart to join with this man in this ministry.

Right after our prayer time together, Otis jumped up and said "Okay! Let's go get a steak!" I learned later that "getting a steak" was something Otis liked to do as a way of celebrating when things went very well! So off we went! We quickly decided, however, it was not likely for us to find a steakhouse in China at that time, so Otis said, "Let's find a seafood place since we are on the seashore." After driving around for about half an hour, our cab driver could not seem to find a seafood place, so we returned to the hotel only to discover that our hotel had an outstanding seafood buffet! We laughed about that and entered the seafood buffet dining room.

It was crowded with Chinese, of course, and had a real long buffet table with all kinds of seafood dishes! Otis and I sat at a table, and the first thing Otis did was bow his head and say, "Let's give thanks!"

Almost immediately, a young Chinese waitress came to our table and said, "I saw you praying! Are you Christians?"

Otis replied, "Yes!"

The waitress said, "Oh, that is wonderful!" She was so excited! Her hands were held together in front of her face almost as if she were praying, and jumping up and down she said, "So am I! I want to serve you! You won't even have to go to the buffet tables unless you want to! I will get you the best of everything!" So then began what would turn out to be one of the highlights of the trip!

The waitress first set up a hot pot on our table, and then she began piling our table with a variety of every kind of seafood imaginable for us to place in the hotpot. Some of the seafood was familiar but much of it was unrecognizable. There was squid, octopus, sea urchin, a multitude of shell fish, crabs, and various other seafood as well as many "veggies" from the sea like seaweed. Among the dishes were metal bowls with covers on them, and it seemed like there was something inside these bowls scratching on the sides! Otis had a bowl in front of him, and I had one in front of me. We both took the covers off simultaneously, and exploding from the bowls were what seemed like an army of small flying shrimp! They went everywhere! We began laughing and grabbing the shrimp from the table and from our clothes and placing them in the hotpot. Tears were streaming from our eyes from all the laughing as we attempted to collect these tiny specimens which were hopping all over the place! After that experience, our meal went very fast as we were hungry and everything seemed to be so good.

During this time together, I saw a side of Otis that was genuine and fun-loving along with his passion for the Chinese people! It was a busy trip but very rewarding as we had this valuable time together, and I was deeply moved by my time with him.

Woody Wooldridge
China Summer Camp Director, BTW

## Otis the Encourager

I remember meeting Otis and Roxann Goodwin at Liberty Baptist College in 1978. Otis and I had mission classes together, and I always remembered him as the old man of the class since he was around 38 years old when he came to Liberty. I met Roxann when I took a job driving a bus route for Thomas Road Baptist Church. She was the secretary in the bus office. But it was not until Otis and Roxann showed up at Central Baptist Church in Vienna, Virginia around 1985 that we really got the opportunity to know them. Of course, anytime you were around Otis and Roxann you just felt at home.

They arrived at CBC at a critical moment in our lives which I know was truly from God. I don't know if Debbie and I would have ever made it to the mission field of Mexico if it had not been for their encouragement. I remember the early days when Debbie was struggling with the thought of moving to another country and taking our young family to a strange unfamiliar place. It was Otis who would take her for a gentle walk and reassure her that everything was going to be alright. As our home church mission's director, Otis not only got us but the entire church excited about world missions. He had a way of encouraging all those with whom he came in touch. The annual mission conferences were full of life as Otis oftentimes led the church in singing the theme song for the conference. To this day I cannot go into the home offices of OTAN/Bridging The World without singing one of our old conference songs *'Til the Whole World Knows* which continues … I will shout and sing of Christ my King, 'til the whole world knows.

During the early years I always suggested for Otis to change the acronym OTAN from Outreach To Asia Nationals to Outreach To All Nations so that our family could go to Mexico as missionaries through the board started by him and Roxann. So, around 1999 he started Bridging The World, and we signed on as the first missionaries.

Otis was always a man of prayer and always encouraged us to take our burdens and needs to the Lord in prayer. He was a friend until the very end, and I know that anyone who knew him feels they had no better friend than Otis Goodwin.

Steve Poston
Missionary to Mexico, BTW

*The complete names of the following individuals have been intentionally withheld for their protection. Their letters have only been lightly edited. Please pray for*

*these real individuals living is Asia and the many other persecuted Christians around the world who risk everything to follow Jesus.*

## He Wants to Meet Us?

It was December 1992 in Siliguri, India that my wife and I along with Rev. Daniel attended a conference named HIMCOI where Nepali Christians from hilly region gathered in huge number. In the midst of the seminar, we got to know that someone from USA wanted to meet me and Rev. Daniel, and we were surprised that someone in that mass would want to meet us.

As we met these strangers, we got to know that these people had come all the way from USA to Nepal and then to India to meet me and Rev. Daniel. Since they couldn't get flight tickets to India, a car was hired, and they travelled 600-700 kms to meet us there in India. We were totally amazed to see these people of God to come all the way to meet us. This was the first time I met Rev. Otis Goodwin.

After a short conversation, we were very blessed and encouraged to learn about OTAN and what it does and finally an agreement on doing the ministry together to extend His kingdom was done right in the conference. Then after, partnership with OTAN mission started and we praise God that this partnership is still continuing for the glory of God. Through this mission many churches have been planted to remote areas of Nepal.

Now, Brother Otis is not with us physically, but I just want to share that he was a man of God and a close brother and mentor to me. His trust and the love for God encourage me always when I am down, and his serving heart is what my family and I have learned. I feel honored to have known this man and be a family to him. He, Sister Roxann and his family will always be a family to me in God. My eyes always fill with tears when I recall his desire to meet me for the last time and how badly I had wished to see him. Though we tried a lot, we couldn't do it due to visa process and rejection, but the time spent with Brother Otis is always fresh in my mind, and I believe we will meet in heaven one day.

We thank God for giving Rev. Otis a vision to teach, equip, and send the people in Asia through OTAN, and this vision is still going on as the partnership is flourishing and bearing fruits in different countries of Asia. Thank you always for building us not only financially, but most important for the trainings, and building us spiritually, and equipping us with the armor of God.

Hari<br>
National Pastor

## The Regions Beyond: Dear Mum Roxann

It has been almost 10 years since I first met you (2008-2018). I can't believe how that first time I met you has lead us so far in ministry. What amazing plans that God has given us to do together, and I am always thankful for that. I am grateful for what you has done for our ladies ministry. The legacies that you left is not only what we can see … ladies who equipped us with the knowledge of the Word of God, but also what we cannot see but is easy to feel … your love for us. Your heart touch our hearts and move our hands to keep doing what we are doing now for the Lord. You may not know that through this ministry there are about seven different tribal groups are equipped and they are from 14 provinces.

Miss W

My family was so poor, and I had to helped my parents to raise my younger brothers and sisters, so I had to stopped my study when I was just in grade 7. I had no idea that someday I can become a teacher, but I do now. I first came to Roxann's training in 2008, and I kept coming every year. I never forgot the lessons of the 10 ladies in the life of Jesus Christ that Roxann taught us. I fall in love with those stories, and it's made me so exciting to sharing it with other ladies in my church. And the more I share, the more I realize that teaching is just simple sharing what you had learn. And that is really true. I started to carry these stories to other villages and teach it. I just fall in love with what I am doing now, and thanks Roxann for your lessons and especially you encouraged me to go out to teach.

Mrs. D

I married when I was 16 years old and have two children, and now I have to taking care of my family. I hadn't gone out of my village before. When I was asked to come to the ladies training [away from my village], I had no idea what it look like and how it's helpful for me. But I am now so exciting and it gave me much idea what I should do and how I can do it. It seem like not really hard to do something for the Lord, and I feel I am more useful for my local church and ministry at my village.

Mrs. L

I sent two ladies from my church to ladies training. I hope that I can send more ladies to this training; it's so helpful for them. As pastor, sometime I don't know how I can help ladies in my church to be more active and faithful in ministry. These two ladies help me to encourage other ladies in my church and start ladies ministry by making friend with other ladies around, sharing what they learn, taking care for each others, praying for each others and bringing some other ladies to church. I am so encouraged by that and hopefully I can send more ladies to OTAN training.

Tribal Pastor

Ladies really need encouragement. They love the fellowship with each others. I love the training once a year that Roxann provide for us. I have been carry her lessons and teaching for about six ladies in my village and felt really proud of it. I hope I can have more time to do that. Thanks, Roxann, for your lesson and your encouragement to all of us.

Mrs. N

We never forget you and your husband. We love you and miss you. Thank you for all you do for us. We pray for you. And please remember to pray for us.

Miss K and mom

I am so blessed to know you and learn from you, especially your love and your care for our ladies make me really appreciative. I am thankful to be involve with this ladies ministry for years, and it's give me much opportunity to serve the low educated ladies who really need help. It's not always easy to do ministry in my country, but with the power of the Holy Spirit in us and the hope for heaven in Christ, there is nothing can stop us to do good works for the Lord, the works that He already prepare for us to do. Thank you for being an example for my life. What you has done is more than enough. I and ladies love you and pray for you.

Miss W

# 9

# God's Faithfulness to the End

> Whereas ye know not what shall be on the morrow. For what is your life? It is even a vapour, that appeareth for a little time, and then vanisheth away.
> James 4:14 KJV

In the spring of 2005, Otis was enjoying good health and had fully recuperated from his long surgical issues. He was back traveling overseas, and the ministry was moving forward at home. We had new home office staff join OTAN. Otis had the blessing of participating in the graduation ceremony of 15 church leaders in Nepal from the OTAN Bible School. Included on this trip was travel to Vietnam and Thailand.

I had been invited to bring a team to Nepal to conduct a training conference for women from various villages. We had 350 women in two different locations, many of which had to walk three to four days to participate in the conferences.

The OTAN building project was moving forward. This two-story addition would triple the square footage at our headquarters. We will always be thankful for the many volunteers who came and worked tirelessly for many hours on this building project and for those who donated funds to complete it.

In December 2004, a devasting tsunami hit southern Thailand. We had a request from our contacts in Thailand to help rebuild a church that had been destroyed. God blessed our efforts, and we were able to raise $125,000 for this project. In April of 2005, Otis went to visit the area and meet with the pastor, and he presented him with funds to start the construction on the church. He traveled back to this area in August to see the progress made on the construction of the church building.

In April 2005 when Otis returned from this last overseas trip, he was having difficulty breathing, shortness of breath, as well as pain in his right side. After x-rays, it was determined that he was experiencing muscle spasms from going to the gym and working out.

In January 2006, Otis' right lung filled with fluid, and he was admitted to the hospital in Winchester, under quarantine for active tuberculosis (TB). They removed 3000 ccs of fluid from his lung. All the tests for TB came back negative. This was an extremely emotional time for our staff and for us as a family. The entire staff had to be tested, as well as our family. Gary and Jana's baby, Jaden, had been staying with us a couple of days a week as Jana was working part time. I was beside myself with worry that she had possibly contracted TB. They did several tests which all came back negative, yet the doctor told us that one could have several tests with negative results before they receive a positive one. Otis came home from the hospital, but we were isolated. Finally, after a while, they decided that we could rule out TB.

In March 2006 he was not any better, and we were sent to the University of Virginia Medical Center in Charlottesville, Virginia. The doctor told us he had pleurisy, and he was told to take Tylenol and that it would be better in a few weeks. During these many CT scans and x-rays, the doctors kept saying that he looked like a patient who had been involved with asbestos, as he had thickening in the lining between his right lung and his abdomen. However, they kept telling us there was no sign of cancer. Memorial Day weekend, his condition worsened, and once again he was admitted to the hospital. They did another CT scan, and it showed the thickening of the lining of his lung had increased even more. His breathing had worsened, and he was on oxygen. They were now saying his lung looked like cancer, most likely from casual contact with asbestos 30 to 35 years prior. They decided to go into his lung from his chest for a biopsy. The test was negative. After this report, the surgeons decided they would go in and scrape the lining of his lung which was going to be a very invasive surgery. They would have to cut out some of his ribs, and we were told it would be a very long, hard recovery.

Just before the surgery, the doctor came to talk with us. They wanted to take another biopsy first. For this biopsy, they would enter the lung from his back. If the results were negative for cancer, they would move forward with the surgery to scrape his lung. If it was positive, they would not do the surgery because there was no cure for this cancer, and the recovery from the surgery would cause too much pain and suffering, if he was able to recover at all. Jana, Gary, and I waited for the biopsy to be completed. About an hour after Otis had gone in, I received a call from the operating room nurse. She told me Otis was doing well, and they were moving forward. I called the office and told the staff the biopsy surgery was moving along.

About an hour later, the doctor came out and called Jana and me into another room. He told us the news; the biopsy was positive for cancer, and there would not be any further surgery. I asked the doctor how long Otis would have, and he just shrugged his shoulders. I was devastated! Never in my life had anything ever affected me as this news did. Not even Otis' death. I completely fell apart. I am sure there are people reading these words who can relate to what I was going through.

So, now what do we do? What do you do when the doctor tells you there is no cure for your cancer and that you only have a short time to live? You PRAY, you cry, you ask God for a miracle. I prayed to God, asking Him for another miracle. Otis had received many miracles through the years, more than I can count. Please God, just one more!

We were transferred to the oncology doctor and made plans for treatment and plans for the future for whatever time the Lord had for Otis. The plan for treatment was chemotherapy, and it was to begin immediately. At that moment, we had a more important family need. Our grandson, Andrew, was graduating from high school, and it was important to us to attend that special time with our family. The chemo was delayed until after we came back from Andrew's graduation.

In June 2006, the chemotherapy started. Otis had good days and days that were not so good, which is the norm for chemo patients. The goal was to stop the growth of the cancer. We were able to continue working in the office, travel to some churches for work, and enjoy time camping in our motorhome. For the last couple of years Otis had been praying for a smooth transition so he could step down as director of OTAN in order for him to take on the role of full-time representative to raise funds and recruit personnel. We had interviewed several men and had even brought a few into the office to work, but nothing had materialized.

In October 2006, after praying and consulting with our doctor, we made the decision to stop the chemo and try a different type of treatment. Through the handful of months of chemotherapy, there was little hope that the treatment was working. At this time, we were encouraged for Otis to try a different type of treatment. It was a weekly treatment called Hydrogen Peroxide IV Therapy and had been used for many years. He was on a high dosage of vitamin B12 and had several detox treatments.

Also in October, we had a meeting with our board of directors, our lawyer, and many donors to discuss Otis' current health and the future of the ministry. It was at this meeting that the board gave me an official title, OTAN's Director of Women's Ministry, to continue in the ministry we had started.

After many long months of construction and dealing with the county, we received our occupancy permit for our new offices. What a day of rejoicing that was to see this beautiful two-story addition completed. On November 17, 2006, OTAN held an open house and dedication ceremony for the new addition to our office. We were overjoyed, and we praised the Lord for what He had accomplished over the many months and the faithfulness of many special people who took time from their own jobs and families to see this day become a reality. Otis and I were presented with a bronze plaque and the naming of the new addition in our honor – the Goodwin Administration Building. How grateful and honored we were for this dedication. Little did we imagine when we first rode up that driveway many years prior that God would have this day in His plans. There were approximately 200 people who attended the dedication, and many memories were shared by the guests. Oh, how we were blessed!

In January 2007, Otis had another CT scan of his lung, and it showed that the cancer had not grown. The doctor even said, "You might say that there is a little improvement." Even though the doctors were not confident that these natural treatments were working, they did encourage us to continue doing what we were doing. He was still on oxygen as needed. Hospice would come out periodically when we needed extra medical support, but when Otis was feeling better they were discharged.

Over the next couple of months Otis started to have pain in his shoulder. They x-rayed the area, did a CT scan and an MRI, and all were negative. So, they diagnosed it as a nerve problem. They put him on more pain medication which did not give him much relief. He continued to work as much as possible and would spend a lot of time on the phone for work as well as talking to family and friends. We were still able to travel some for speaking engagements at churches, but Otis would often sit in a chair to address the congregations. The cancer had taken a toll on his body.

Exciting things continued to happen within our family. Our grandson Corey Bailey, arrived home from a year in Iraq. What a joy to be able to travel to Maine and see him as he came off that plane well and safe. We thanked God for keeping him safe that past year. On the way to the airport we stopped to purchase an American flag, and when Otis saw Corey, he wrapped the flag around him and gave him a big bear hug. How proud we were of our grandson. Jana and Gary presented us with our ninth grandchild, Josalyn Mae Moritz. She was named after Otis' mother, and she joined big sister Jaden. I have always been grateful to the Lord that Otis was able to see all our grandchildren born.

In May, our grandson, Michael Bailey, who had battled leukemia was now graduating from Liberty University, and we were able to attend this special time with our family. A week later Michael and Rebekah got married, and Otis had the privilege of marrying them. Michael was our first grandchild to get married. It was during this time that Otis started to fail. He was not feeling well at all. When we returned home from the wedding, we discovered he had pneumonia. He was having more difficulty breathing and was on oxygen full time. I went and bought a lift chair because he was not able to lie down.

He began complaining that his feet felt numb, and he started to fall periodically. Our grandson, Lee Bailey, came from Maine to stay with us and help out. One morning Otis tried to get up from the chair, and he slid to the floor. He was not able to stand or walk. We had to call 911 for help to get him back into the chair. I called the doctor, and he told me Otis had to come back into the hospital to see what was going on. The doctor suspected that the cancer had gone to his spine. When they did the MRI, it showed a large tumor on his spine, and he became paralyzed from the waist down. This came on very quickly. The doctor said he probably wouldn't live more than a week.

The doctor said he would keep Otis in the hospital as long as was needed, but I wanted to take him home to care for him. Hospice was already back supporting us, and they arranged to have a hospital bed set up in our bedroom by the time we left the hospital. He was sedated but able to receive many visitors and was still able to talk on the phone.

He had a special phone call with all our grandsons. He knew that Corey and Kara as well as Joshua and Becky were planning to marry in the near future. He shared with Joshua and Corey their responsibilities as a husband.

Julie flew down with lobsters and clams from Maine. On July 15, we celebrated Otis' 68th birthday. He enjoyed the lobsters and clams. You can take the man out of Maine, but you can't take Maine out of the man!

I was still doing some accounting for OTAN, and I brought my work home, working in our bedroom. I knew "that" time was drawing near. He was sleeping most of the time, but periodically he would wake up and say to me, "Come here. We need to talk." I would go over to him, and he would say to me, "What are we going to do?" I responded and said, "Otis, you are going to go to heaven, and I am going to be okay." He would say, "Okay," and go back to sleep. This conversation occurred over and over. He never talked about dying or what he wanted for a funeral. One thing he said to me was, I want you to continue on in the ministry, and I don't want you to live alone. I promised him I would continue in the ministry, but I told him I couldn't promise that I would not live alone.

Jana, Gary, Michael, Rebekah, Julie, Lee and I were all present when the angels in heaven escorted Otis home on July 19, 2007.

*He who comes prepared will go away satisfied.*
*Otis S. Goodwin*

A few months prior, I had gone to the funeral home in Winchester and called the funeral home in Gardiner, Maine to make preparations for the funeral and for Otis to be flown to Maine.

We had a memorial service at Capital Baptist Church in Annandale, Virginia. This was the church we attended from the first day we moved back to Virginia in 1985, and Steve Reynolds was our pastor. There was a big crowd at this service. Dr. Jerry Kroll shared about the relationship between Otis and the national pastors; Dr. Jerry Mick shared about the relationship between Otis and the board of directors; and our dear and faithful friend, the late Bill Hurley, shared about Otis' relationship with the local church mission ministry. Pastor Jim Bitner shared about Otis' support in starting the mission program in his church. Steve Poston spoke about Otis' encouragement to a young couple just going out to the mission field, and Lily Hidalgo spoke about our friendship. Michael shared about his relationship with his grandfather and Jana with her relationship with her father. Pastor Steve shared about his relationship as our pastor. It was an uplifting service with many tears and a lot of laughter.

After the service in Virginia, Jana, Gary, and I flew to Maine to have the funeral at Calvary Bible Baptist Church. Again, we had a blessed service with Jana and Michael speaking again as well as Julie sharing about her relationship with her father and our grandson Lee sharing about his relationship with his grandfather. Pastor Jerry Wright spoke as a friend and our pastor, and Pastor Steve flew to Maine and did the committal service. Our grandson, Joshua, gave the invitation at the close of the service with a very clear presentation of the Gospel's plan of salvation and what it means to become a Christian. Otis is buried in the Whitefield Cemetery with his mother, father, sister, and brother-in-law and has since been joined by his great grandson, Boaz Otis Bailey. After the funeral, we went to the airport in Portland to fly back to Virginia only to find out that our flight had been canceled. We took the bus to Boston and waited and waited for our flight to leave for home, only to learn late that night that all flights were canceled, and so we spent the night in the airport in Boston.

Once we arrived back to Jana's home, I left to go home to Winchester alone to begin a new journey without the person who had been by my side since the eighth grade. As I drove up that long Bethany Hill Drive, my life flashed in front of my eyes. I remembered the first time we drove up that driveway, and I thought about all that had taken place in our lives while living on the hill. The office was closed, and I was going into an empty house, alone.

I was entering a new chapter in my life. *How am I going to make it?*

*"Because He lives, I can face tomorrow."*

My life has been enriched since meeting Otis Goodwin in the late 1990s when he stopped by the church and asked if he could speak with the pastor. Like so many other pastors over the years, I found myself speaking to a man I had never met about training nationals in Asia. He was full of passion and had a zeal that was uncompromising. He went on to challenge our church to get involved.

Not long after, Crosspoint Church began to support OTAN, and before I knew it, he had me sitting on the board of directors and soon after the chairman of the board. During this time, we became extremely close friends and co-laborers in the Lord's kingdom.

As we know, Otis' illness came to a place where he had to step down as executive director of the organization. I will never forget that day when I approached him in his office with Roxann and informed him it was time to rest from his labors. Due to his illness and medication, it became very difficult for him mentally to process clearly and make decisions. I have done many difficult things in my 35 years in ministry, and that was without a doubt the most difficult. There were a lot of tears that day between Otis, Roxann, and me, but Otis knew the end had come, and he accepted it as the Lord's timing. He graciously stepped down immediately and threw all his support during his last days behind me and OTAN.

I was fortunate to go with him on his last trip. Together we visited numerous churches in

Pennsylvania asking pastors to support OTAN and for them to allow Otis to come and share about the ministry. I knew in my heart he would not be healthy enough to do that, but it did not slow him down! He truly believed he would have the strength and stamina. He was very ill during our travels, but he never complained. He just kept eating more dark chocolate that he claimed would make him better; we both chuckled. I knew the end was near, and he did also. But outwardly he would never express it, relying on God to heal him until the very end.

I learned a lot on that last trip with Otis. I saw what perseverance and determination was all about. A man sick and dying yet serving God with all he had left! I saw passion for God's work that had I never seen before or since. I saw a man demonstrate faith like I had never seen before or since.

I remember asking him one night before we went to sleep, "Otis, how long can you keep doing this? You are so sick and in pain."

And he answered, "Until I am with Jesus!"

And he did just that, to the very end!

We also traveled together numerous times to Asia, and I saw firsthand his love for the people of Asia. It was incredible how he showed his love and compassion to the people. He hugged them, prayed for them, engaged them, cried with them, laughed with them, and most importantly, did ministry with them! He had such a love that it cut through cultural barriers, and I got to witness that happen right in front of me. People who could not speak the same language quickly became united through love and mission. It was contagious, and anyone who knew Otis knows what I mean.

After the passing of Otis, I traveled from Bangor, Maine, one week a month to work in the OTAN office for a year as the interim executive director. These were times which enriched me personally as the OTAN team and the board of directors pulled together. When a founder passes away, an organization is at a crossroads. People at large, OTAN missionaries, supporters, and staff were wondering what was going to happen. Would we go forward? Would we keep the vision and Otis' passion alive? By God's grace we were able to move forward, and the vision has remained the same.

For those taking time to read this book, God bless you for your love for OTAN and Asia.

Dr. Jerry Mick<br>
Senior Pastor at Crosspoint Church<br>
Banger, Maine

**Tears From My Eyes**

Sitting on the rough tile floor
Listening to the pitter patter of the rain
Hitting the tin roof.
Girls running around looking for me
Telling me that my mom was outside
Waiting to talk to me
I walked out the door to see what was the matter
All she said was that my Grampa was dead
I yelled "no" and fell in her arms
As I was thinking about the good times I had with him
I knew, some day I will see him again.
I walked back inside and told my friends
They all supported me during that
Sad, sad time.
I know I will see him again up in Heaven
I still think of him
When I do tears start falling from my eyes

Kristina Bailey, age 13

## I Am Poem

I am loving and kind
I wonder how long forever is
I hear my mom and dad
I see love and kindness
I want a dog
I am loving and kind

I pretend to be a singer
I feel loved by mom and dad
I touch the moon
I worry that it could be my last day
I am loving and kind

I understand kindness
I say that God is real
I dream that Bumpa is still alive
I try to be good
I hope that I see Bumpa in Heaven
I am loving and kind

Josalyn Mae Moritz, age 10

# 10

## A New Tomorrow

> Have not I commanded thee? Be strong and of a good courage; be not afraid, neither be thou dismayed: for the Lord thy God is with thee whithersoever thou goest.
>
> Joshua 1:9 KJV

After the emotional, uplifting, and blessed memorial services for Otis in both Virginia and Maine and then the long journey trying to get home, I was exhausted. I came home to an empty house and a new role ... a widow. What was I going to do? How was I going to do it? What was expected of me? How was I going to manage everything?

Pastor Steve often mentioned that when we go through a crisis or challenge in life, we "either get bitter or better." I knew for the sake of my family, the ministry, and myself that I didn't want to get bitter. I knew my life would never be the same again. People told me that time helps with the ache, and that is true. But nothing takes the pain away completely other than the Lord's comfort, presence, and peace.

I was overwhelmed with the prayers of so many people who sent notes, cards, special gifts, and financial support. Our supporting churches were more than gracious to me with their continued support. Many who have visited the OTAN/BTW home office know how far the property is from the main highway, surrounded with woods and no neighbors within sight. It was a lonely time after all the staff went home every night. One of the greatest blessings was when Reston Bible Church and Capital Baptist Church provided the finances to have a security system put into my home. What peace I had when I came home from the office at night or when I returned from a trip and was able to turn on the security system.

The OTAN/BTW Board of Directors continued to be faithful and see that our ministries continued to move forward. A major encouragement to me and to our staff was when Dr. Jerry Mick, a board member, committed to come to the OTAN office one week a month for a whole year to move the ministry forward after Otis died. The staff were faithful in keeping the office running smoothly.

I went back into the office to work full time as I tried to adjust to living alone while moving forward. My family continued to grow. Corey and Kara were planning a December 2007 wedding. Joshua and Becky were planning a February 2008 wedding. I knew without a doubt in 2008 I would have the privilege of becoming a great-grandmother. What an exciting event to look forward to.

During the time when we knew Otis' condition was such that he might not have a lot of time to live, he kept telling me that I had to continue on in the ministry. Since the beginning of OTAN I had gone on several trips, training and ministering to women in several of the countries targeted by OTAN. Of course, now I had a title too – director of women's ministry. I guess you could say that I hit the ground running. I immediately started to make plans for overseas travel. My first trip was to Vietnam and Cambodia in February 2008 and then to Nepal and Thailand in August and September of 2008. Little did I realize that I would have such a busy year.

I returned from my trip to Vietnam and Cambodia on February 29, 2008. My friend Lily traveled with me. It was a safe, positive, and heartwarming trip. We had the privilege of teaching 26 women. Thirteen had never been involved in any type of training. There were some women who came that I had met 11 years prior. Many had pictures of me with them on that last visit. We had several pastors' wives in this group who told me that Otis had visited in their homes. It was a very emotional time. One of the ladies who came was a tribal lady who I had met the first time I went to Vietnam with Otis. Her dad was a pastor, and she traveled with him teaching children. To this day she is still working with children in her village. Otis had given her money to buy teaching tools for her work.

We always made these training sessions like a retreat for these ladies. We would have crafts for them that related to one of the lessons. The ladies really enjoyed getting into these projects, and it was fun to watch them laugh and enjoy themselves. This was a special time of fellowship for us and for the ladies. We always encouraged the women to go back to their village and teach other women what they had learned at the retreat. This was the foundation of OTAN – Nationals Reaching Nationals. When I told the ladies I would return to Vietnam in 2009, they were excited and said they would come again and bring a friend. It appeared the Vietnamese government was giving the church some freedom, but after we left, we found out that one of our pastors was arrested and interrogated, after which he was finally released.

In August I traveled to Nepal for women's training. What a blessing to see many friends and pastors who knew Otis and had been praying for him for many months. Otis always had a desire to return one more time but that was not in God's plan. We had 125 women participate in this women's training. Nepal was the only country where I had problems traveling. When people ask me if I ever got scared, I tell them about the rat story in Cambodia. Then, I tell them that I was always stressed traveling in Nepal around the Himalayan Mountains. There were no guard rails, and we rode in vans traveling at high speed around corners nearly missing big trucks. We also faced washed-out roads. I decided when I had to travel outside of Katmandu I was going to fly! I discovered that this was not less stressful, but at least it was quicker. I could be scared for 4-5 hours in a van; or I could be scared for 30 minutes sitting behind the pilots as I watched them fly between the mountains. I could see their every move. Flying between the Himalayan Mountains was such a beautiful sight! The pastors were always very gracious to make sure I was on the right flight and that there was always someone to meet me.

I remember the first flight I took from Pokhara back to Katmandu. We started our descent to land at the airport, but I did not see a runway to land on anywhere. The plane landed in a cow pasture, the cows scattered, and the mud flew. This was the first time I saw nationals walking to the plane turning their prayer wheels. These wheels had a cylinder of paper with prayers written inside ... prayers to the Hindu gods for safety on the flight. They needed to hear about the Living God who hears our prayers, answers our prayers, and keeps us safe. One time when Otis was scheduled to fly on a similar flight, the plane before his flight hit a radio tower, crashed, and everyone was killed. The pastor who was waiting for him in Katmandu thought Otis was on that flight. God has our lives in His hands.

In September, I traveled to Thailand and then up towards the border of Laos. Laos was and still currently is a restricted access country, and we were not allowed to train inside this country. There was much persecution going on in Laos. The women were allowed a visa to travel into Thailand for a certain number of days if they stayed within a certain distance of the border. There was much persecution going on in Laos. We had three days of amazing training.

The husband of one of the attending ladies had been ambushed and killed coming home from a church meeting a few weeks prior to the training. His only crime was that he was a pastor. These women and their families lived in deep poverty and severe persecution. It was a very humbling experience to share this time with them. I lived in a beautiful home; I had more clothes in my closet than I would ever wear; my husband had loved me dearly; I lived in a country where I could go to church whenever I wanted. I knew traveling 13 or 14 long hours by plane, traveling another three hours by plane, and then another three hours by van to finally arrive at the training site was minor compared to what these ladies go through just to survive daily. Add to this the fact that they could very well be interrogated by authorities when they returned home for being in Thailand. We had been told to expect 30 women to attend, but 50 showed up to the training. One lady arrived with her newborn baby wearing no clothes, just a diaper. Thankfully we were able to buy the baby clothes before they returned home. I was told that the women would not be able to carry any of the material back with them into Laos for fear that their belongings would be searched upon return. However, I was told that some women would secretly carry material on their bodies nonetheless!

That year turned out to be quite a year. Not only did I make three trips overseas, but I was invited to visit 12 of my supporting churches, as well as a new church in Missouri. I traveled all over the eastern United States. Sometimes I flew, and other times I drove. I was really quite overwhelmed by all the invitations to come and speak and share what my life was about now on my own and what the OTAN Women's Ministry was doing in these different countries. I stayed with many friends who Otis and I had met through the years … faithful prayer supporters who still pray for me to this day.

As many of you know, when you lose a loved one you always experience difficult "firsts" – the first Christmas, Thanksgiving, wedding anniversary, etc. One of my most difficult "firsts" was when I was flying home from my first overseas trip. All of a sudden, I realized Otis was not going to be there to meet me at the airport. By the time I landed, I was a total wreck. It was always a special time for us when one of us returned home, and the other was there to meet them. One time when I came home our bed was covered with new clothes for me. He loved shopping for me. Other times when he was due home, he would call me and tell me to plan a getaway. It might be for just a day or two, but it was a special time to be together. It was a struggle to adjust to this new way of life without him.

## Jesus Told Us to "Occupy Till I Come" Luke 19:13

My family was growing; I welcomed my first great-grandson, Ashton Bailey, and I was looking forward to another great-grandbaby due in January 2009.

I continued to work in the OTAN office when I was not traveling and was planning my travel schedule for 2009. In January I took my first trip to Russia. Now I know what most people thought when I told them I was going to Russia in January. Who in their right mind would go to Russia in January? Well, I would. I decided I needed to dress warm, so I splurged and bought a coat from L.L. Bean that was good for 20 degrees below zero. I was very glad to have it, and it kept me warm. Ice and snow were everywhere, but people move forward with their lives no matter the weather, even having yard sales in 20 degrees below zero weather. I did several sessions on encouragement from the Psalms. I met several people who knew Otis, and I visited a church that was started by Al and Joy Doomy, as well as a home for children called Hope For Life that they started and is still functioning today.

In July my granddaughter Kristina and I traveled to China with a Bridging The World summer camp team. Otis had promised her that he would take her, but, of course, he didn't live long enough to fulfill that promise. So, I was very pleased to have her travel with me. It was during this time that people were sick with the swine flu. All passengers traveling to China had to be screened by health authorities and have their temperature taken upon arrival. If we or anyone sitting near us had a temperature, we had to be quarantined five to seven days in a Chinese hotel. Needless to say, we sent out an urgent prayer request. God was good, and we all arrived healthy and stayed healthy.

While in China, the second anniversary of Otis going to heaven came and went. It was another very emotional time, but a time rejoicing in how God was using the ministry of BTW too. I taught conversational English to a group of Chinese children 12 to 13 years old. Little did I know that in 2018, nine years later, my daughter Jana and granddaughter Jaden would travel with BTW teaching conversational English to a group of Chinese boys and girls too. At this time, seven of my grandchildren had had the opportunity to travel overseas and see the ministry at work firsthand.

My family was doing well. My son-in-law Gary had a great trip to Nepal and was able to see the OTAN ministry there. My grandson Michael and his wife Rebekah joined the staff of Capital Baptist Church as their youth pastor.

In the fall of 2009, I traveled to Vietnam, Cambodia, and Nepal. This year was a fruitful year for the women's ministry. We trained 55 women from Laos, 44 women in Vietnam, 40 women in Cambodia, and 99 women in Nepal. This was my second trip into Cambodia. Virginia from Vietnam traveled with me. We went by bus and had to cross the Mekong River on a barge. Many of the bridges that had been destroyed during a previous war were never rebuilt. We were on a big bus maxed out with people going across the river on the barge. I kept thinking, "Lord show me how to get out of this bus if we should start to sink." As usual, He kept me safe and kept the bus from sinking.

As 2009 was coming to an end, I was preparing to go to Russia for the second time in January 2010. My friend Louise was traveling with me. For some crazy reason I seemed to schedule my trips to Russia in January. We had heard it was 30 to 35 degrees below zero, and they just had two feet of snow. But I was ready to go because I had my Russian coat!

As I have mentioned previously, the Lord had done many miracles in our lives and in ministries, and He was about to perform another miracle. What a blessing to know that the Lord hears our prayers and answers. I was about to find myself in a situation where I needed a miracle, and I needed it in a hurry.

When we arrived in Russia, little did I know I was about to spend the first five hours in the Russian airport police station. I went through security without any issues, and I picked up my bags and started towards security and x-ray. There was a huge crowd pushing and shoving, and as I started to go through security, I still had my shoulder bag on. The guard motioned for me to take it off and put it on the machine. I remember seeing a man close to me as we both were picking up our bags. I met my contact person, and we put our bags in her van and started out of the airport. All of a sudden, I realized I didn't have my shoulder bag. My bag had my passport (which of course had my visa stamped in it), my hearing aids (I didn't wear them when I was flying because of too much noise), $5 in cash, my cell phone, and some of my curriculum that was already translated. We turned around and went back into the airport immediately, but my bag was nowhere to be found. It didn't take long for several people to become involved in the search.

Needless to say, I was in a very precarious situation. I did have sense enough to call the U.S. Consulate. The agent I talked with told me they could issue me a new passport, but the problem would be the visa. The Russian government might not be willing to give me another visa, and if that happened, I could have trouble leaving the country as well as traveling throughout Russia. I was only going to be in Vladivostok one day as I would be traveling to three different areas of Russia training women. The next four hours were spent filling out reports in English with my contact person translating them into Russian and repeating the whole story over and over as new officers came to listen to my story. The entire security department was very kind and had great sympathy for me.

Finally, there was a call from airport security. The U.S. Consulate called the airport and said that a man had just come to the consulate to return my bag stating he had picked it up by mistake. Wow! A very quick answer to prayer. When I finally arrived at my hotel room, I called the consulate and was told to come to their office the next morning. The U.S. agent had gone through my bag and nothing was missing, not even the $5.

The next morning, I arrived at the consulate to pick up my bag. The agent said I didn't have any more pages in my passport. Here I go again. I knew it was going to be close, but I thought I could get by until I returned home from this trip. He was very nice and said, "I will put more pages in your passport, and I will do it for free." Then he questioned me, asking if I had registered with U.S. Immigration to let them know I was traveling outside the country. I told him I hadn't. He informed me that they did not want to track me, but that if I was found dead on the side of the road, they would know who to call! Food for thought!

We traveled to three areas of Russia and taught a total of 115 women. We had the opportunity to share in one church I had been in the previous year, and several of the ladies came again this year. God provided many blessings over the years. One specifically I will always remember. Our ministry manager asked me to purchase a Bible for a young Russian man who was a new Christian. His girlfriend would be attending one of the trainings. I had no name, nor did I know his girlfriend. At the second training a young girl came to me and said she knew I was carrying a Bible for her boyfriend and that he was coming that day to pick it up. I was so excited, but I had to go back to the hotel to pick up the Bible. My translator went with me to the hotel. My room was on the third floor. After picking up the Bible, we got into the elevator and it started moving down, but then it stopped. Here we were pounding on the door of the elevator for quite a while praying for God to work another quick miracle to get the elevator moving. Finally, it started working, and we landed on the first floor. I decided to walk up and down the stairs from that time on. Satan was trying to intervene, but he failed. What a day of rejoicing when this young man arrived, and I was able to give him a Bible. He hugged it to his heart and said, "I am so grateful for this special gift. I love this Bible." I had many times of such sweet blessings.

My first trip back to Nepal after Otis died was another one of these times. I was pondering what I could do with all of Otis' clothes, and I decided I would take his shirts and ties to Nepal and give them to all the pastors who were going to be in the training. I had enough shirts and ties for each pastor, and it was exciting to see the smiles on their faces as they each took home one of Otis' shirts and ties. Otis loved these men dearly, and they loved him. Many had tears in their eyes as they received these clothes.

Over the next few years I continued to travel with other ladies to each of these countries, many times, two to three times each year with more than one country each trip. My family continued to grow too. My great grandchildren were arriving, and by the end of 2010, five had been born. What a joy and a blessing for this new generation.

**Twenty-five Years and Counting, 2011**

The Lord had allowed OTAN to come a long way from that austere start in that little two-level rented townhouse with a $750 start-up budget. The foundation was laid – "Nationals Reaching Nationals" – and 25 years later that was still our goal. We were supporting approximately 150 Christian workers in Asia, multiple orphanages, and other ministries. We were in our new office facility sitting on 50 acres of land on a beautiful hillside in Winchester, Virginia.

The year 2013 brought change in my life personally. After Otis had died years earlier, Jana and Gary came to me and told me I would eventually live with them when the Lord's timing was right. Well, that time arrived, and in the spring of 2013, I moved with them to Fitchburg, Massachusetts. Gary took a position as pastor at City United Church in Lunenburg, Massachusetts. I had lived alone in Winchester since Otis had died, and the Lord had given me peace during those years. But I was ready to move on, and the Lord provided just the right home for us all.

The Lord has blessed me multiple times through the years. One of the greatest joys in my life was when my daughter Kim traveled with me to Thailand, and we brought women out of the country of Laos. Kim taught and led crafts with the ladies. What a pleasure it was to see her step up and interact with these precious ladies and to serve with her in missions.

I had a tough time on this trip physically. I was taking Kim touring in Bangkok, and we were at the floating market. We were riding in a canoe-type boat alongside the canal, and there were markets selling all kinds of items on both sides. Sandie Powell, Kim and I, along with a young medical intern from Liberty University, were in the boat. I was the last to climb up onto the cement walkway, and as I started the boat rocked. I fell forward skinning my right leg from my knee to my ankle. I was bleeding and in much pain. One of the workers came and started putting bandages on my leg. I guess it must have happened before as they seemed prepared. On our way back to the hotel, we found a pharmacy where I purchased supplies to take care of my leg. I was also able to buy an antibiotic.

You can buy most antibiotics in these countries without a prescription. I really had done a job on my leg, and I still had to fly up to the border of Laos and ride in a van for another two hours to reach the training site. Plus, I had three days of teaching ahead of me. On top of that, I had to reverse all this travel and fly back to the United States. I not only was in a bad situation with my leg, but I started having a toothache. By God's grace I was able to complete the training and survived the trip home. My son-in-law, Gary, picked me up at the airport and took me to urgent care. I ended up with a staph infection, and it took several weeks to heal. Sandie was a real trooper and took Kim shopping and touring from that time on, as I was really struggling with just trying to survive teaching. I was not looking forward to the 20 hours it would take to arrive home. This was the very first time I was ever injured in all my travels.

In 2016, my daughter, Jana, and my 12-year-old granddaughter, Jaden, traveled with me to Russia along with Sandie Powell. Thank goodness I thought ahead and didn't plan it for the month of January this time. This was Jaden's first overseas trip, and she was a trooper. She loved the travel, the ladies, the food, and, of course, the ladies just loved her.

The women were moved emotionally when they realized that I had my daughter and granddaughter with me for the training. They kept saying with tears in their eyes, "We don't have a Christian heritage." The majority of the women were first generation Christians. I was overwhelmed and realized how the Lord blessed me with the opportunity to have Jana and Jaden serve with me together in missions. Jana and Sandie shared during a two-hour Question & Answer session on the experiences of being a pastor's wife, the role of women in the church, and raising children in the ministry.

> *My time in Russia was a great adventure. One thing that amazed me was that the people had so little, yet they always wanted to give. The memories made were*

*ones that will be looked back on and remembered. I can't wait to experience more great adventures and tell more people about my Savior!*

*Jaden Moritz*

Since that trip, Jaden has traveled to Guatemala three times and China for four weeks serving the Lord.

## A New Season in Life

> For since the beginning of the world men have not heard, not perceived by the ear, neither hath the eye seen, Oh God, beside thee, what he hath prepared for him that waiteth for him.
>
> Isaiah 64:4 KJV

How true these words are as I look back over my formative years as a young girl growing up in a little farm community in Whitefield, Maine. Sheltered from the world, I had no idea there was a big, wide world out there; a world that needs to hear that Jesus Christ loves them and died for them. The Lord provided for me to travel to many different countries, over 50 times since 1985. I have met hundreds of the most precious people on this earth. I have prayed with them, cried with them, laughed with them, and shared the gospel of Jesus Christ with them. I have traveled with them, I have visited in their homes, and they have cooked meals for me. I have become part of these women's lives as a mother, an aunt, and a sister in Christ. These women have come from areas of the world where they have been taught that their only purpose in life is to be used and abused. Many are among the poorest of the poor in the world today.

God has given me a full life, and at this season of life, it is time to pass the mantle to the next generation. My daughters, my grandsons, my granddaughters and now many of my little great-grandchildren have accepted the Lord as their Savior.

I pray this story will be an encouragement to the future generations of OTAN/BTW staff as they pick up the mantle to carry forward these ministries, as well as a way to encourage believers to have a vision to serve the Lord in whatever mission the Lord is leading them – to move forward, pray, and seek godly council. The mission God gave to us is not yet finished. We are to be busy about this task until God takes us home. As the work and workers continue on, may they always bring honor and glory to Jesus Christ.

> Go ye therefore, and teach all nations, baptizing them in the name of the Father, and of the Son, and of the Holy Ghost: Teaching them to observe all things whatsoever I have commanded you: and lo, I am with you always, even unto the end of the world. Amen.
> Matthew 28:19-20 KJV

**Otis, the Pattern Setter**

Everyone who knew Otis Goodwin knew he was one of a kind. For me, he was a pattern setter. The pattern Otis left me started in the early 1990s when he came to Truth Baptist Church in Jefferson, Maine. Thinking back on it, I'm surprised he bothered to stop in at all to a church our size on a weekday. There were no cars in the parking lot. But his decision changed my life. He cast a vision that day to the pastor and me. (I was the youth pastor.) He expanded our capacity to think that we could have an impact on world missions. At the time, we were contributing $3,500 annually to missions. Otis offered to help us. He took us by the hand and worked with our church step by step. He taught us how to form a mission's committee, how to implement faith promise giving, how to have a mission's conference, how to choose which missionaries to support, and so on. In just a few years, our church of 80 people moved forward to trust God for big things by first, as Otis preached, giving ourselves to the Lord. The church's missions giving soon jumped to $60,000 through faith promise giving.

It wasn't long before I felt called into full-time missions to Russia. The first person Joy and I called was Otis. He asked me to consider Vladivostok. The city borders China and North Korea which fit the OTAN strategy well. It wasn't long before we were on deputation. The stories are endless about how the Lord provided wisdom and encouragement, godly advice, and much needed humor along the way through Otis. Our family was privileged to be in several conferences with Roxann and Otis, and they were our example, our pattern. Many of us still talk about Otis' sermons and illustrations from those days. His passion for the lost was moving; I mean, it *really moved* people to change their lives. Several people were called out of that little church in Maine to follow the Lord in full-time service and are still serving to this day. It's amazing to think about the influence of this one man who was yielded to the Spirit of God.

He pushed me and held my hand at the same time as I went to Russia. When I thought my vision for that ministry was big enough, he challenged me to think bigger and trust God for more. There's so much I could say and want to say about Otis and his strong, unassuming wife, Roxann – his rock – who quietly supported her husband and followed him to the ends of the earth for the sake of the gospel.

They always included our girls, loved them, and considered them part of the ministry as we did. It is no coincidence that our three adult daughters have surrendered to missions and are serving the Lord with their husbands. Our two youngest daughters who are still at home are very much involved in our ministry, and we are very blessed to see their hearts are tender toward missions and service.

The Goodwins sowed deep seeds into our lives, and we seek to follow that pattern as we move forward. The shoes are not to be filled, but the footprints they've left are always before me. I praise God for such a passionate and faithful man as Otis Goodwin and for such a Spirit-filled and surrendered woman as his dear wife, Roxann. It has been one of the greatest blessings of my life to know them.

Al Doomy<br>Executive Director, OTAN and BTW

## MacArthur's move to OTAN

My wife and I met Otis and Roxann while attending Liberty Baptist College (now known as Liberty University) in 1980. We were all from Maine, and it seemed that people from the same state would connect with each other. Otis worked as a security guard for the college, so I would see him while he was on duty. My wife, Eloise, taught a first grade Sunday School class which their youngest daughter, Jana, attended. Each week when Roxann came to pick up her daughter, she and Eloise would briefly chat.

In 1983 I graduated from the college and my family moved to South Liberty, a small town in southern Maine, to take a position at the South Liberty Baptist Church. This town was about 20 miles from where Otis and Roxann lived. We continued to stay in contact with each other over the course of several years. One year, Jana attended South Liberty Baptist Academy where I taught. During this time, Otis and Roxann were starting their mission project, and the following year, the Goodwins moved to Virginia.

In 1987, Eloise and I moved to Lewiston, Maine where I took a position as an assistant to the pastor of Auburn Baptist Church. When Otis was on deputation in Maine, he would visit me at the church and tell me about Outreach To Asia Nationals.

We would spend some time together, go to lunch, and Otis would ask me to come see the work in Winchester, Virginia.

In 2004, Otis called one day and talked to Eloise because I was away working a second shift job. Otis told her that he wanted to talk to me about working at the home office in Winchester, VA. Eloise relayed the message when I came home from work, and I told her that I would return the call eventually, but I was not interested in being a missionary with OTAN. Eloise reminded me to call Otis on several occasions over the next few days.

One night while I was at work, I was thinking about the job I was doing and wondered if it was what I should be doing for the rest of my life. I had been praying and asking God if working this secular job was what I went to college to do. I had also been praying and asking the Lord to open the door and allow me to serve in another church to benefit from my training. The thought came to me that maybe Otis' call was God beginning to open a door back into Christian service. I finally called Otis a few nights later, and we talked about me coming to Winchester to fill the need for a property and facility manager. As the conversation progressed, I told Otis that I thought I could do that. Otis replied, "Now brother, you understand we are a faith-based ministry."

I said, "Yes," and he repeated the statement again. I told Otis, "Yes, I understand. You want to hire me, but I have to pay my own way."

Otis replied, "That is right, brother."

In 2004, between Christmas and the new year, Eloise and I visited the Goodwins at their home in Winchester. We discussed the needs for the ministry and what had to be done to get accepted by the board of directors. In the spring of 2005, we were accepted by the board and started the process of deputation. Deputation went well for about a year. Then, due to no openings to present the ministry in churches, it stopped. The Goodwins were in Maine visiting family so Eloise and I went to see them and discuss the situation. Otis inquired if moving to Winchester and finding a part-time job while working at the office and continuing to do deputation from there was an option. I told Otis that we had been praying about that very thing. God had spoken separately to Eloise and me during a church service and encouraged us to step out in faith and prepare to move to Virginia.

In August of 2006, we made minor repairs on our house, and listed it in September. By the end of November, it was under contract and closed on December 29. After a short stop to visit family in Connecticut, we arrived in Winchester on January 3, 2007.

Once we moved to Winchester, I took a job driving a school bus for Frederick County to supplement our income and earn health insurance benefits until our support level was what it needed to be. Eloise worked in the office helping with receipting, answering the phone, and planning and preparing meals for the various meetings at the office. She also helped with housekeeping and any other projects she could perform. She performed these tasks until she developed health issues that made it impossible for her to continue with these office duties.

Arthur MacArthur<br>
Ministry Manager for Laos, OTAN

**Additional notes from Roxann**

Arthur's responsibilities at OTAN were to take care of the buildings and property. He renovated the older part of the office building. He maintained the outside of the facility and grounds which included snow removal during winter and maintaining the roadway. He set up a protocol for how the property was to be maintained. He helped to totally renovate the residences on the property and changed the basement of the home into a self-contained efficiency apartment for missionaries to use when in Winchester.

He also realized there were tasks in the office that the ministry needed performed but no one was performing them. To help the ministry run well, he learned how to perform low level IT work on the server and various computer and printer systems. He learned how to solve many challenges within the computer program that was used to track all the donations and donor data. He organized and managed a team of volunteers to ensure that various newsletters were printed and mailed in a timely manner.

Over time, Arthur learned the many tasks that keep the office running smoothly and stepped into the role of manager while still performing facilities and IT management.

In 2008, he was asked to become the ministry manager for the country of Laos. This task required him to present this ministry in various churches in order to raise funds to support the national pastors as well as support the various trainings for the national pastors and workers of Laos. He and Eloise organized teams, developed training materials, and traveled to Thailand to perform various seminars to train and equip the nationals and provide the materials they could use in the areas within Laos where Americans are not able to go. Arthur has been integral in keeping the ministry moving forward.

An executive director once stated that Arthur's role at OTAN was, "Doing what others don't, won't, and can't."

# Epilogue

My parents, Otis and Roxann Goodwin, have truly been on an *Incredible Journey*. In this book you have read story after story of how God took ordinary people and used them to do extraordinary things. This fact never ceases to amaze me. As I read this book, over and over my mind went to Hebrews 11, the faith chapter of the Bible.

> And what shall I more say? for the time would fail me to tell of Gedeon, and of Barak, and of Samson, and of Jephthae; of David also, and Samuel, and of the prophets: Who through faith subdued kingdoms, wrought righteousness, obtained promises, stopped the mouths of lions. Quenched the violence of fire, escaped the edge of the sword, out of weakness were made strong, waxed valiant in fight, turned to flight the armies of the aliens. Women received their dead raised to life again: and others were tortured, not accepting deliverance; that they might obtain a better resurrection: And others had trial of cruel mockings and scourgings, yea, moreover of bonds and imprisonment: They were stoned,

they were sawn asunder, were tempted, were slain with the sword: they wandered about in sheepskins and goatskins; being destitute, afflicted, tormented; (Of whom the world was not worthy:) they wandered in deserts, and in mountains, and in dens and caves of the earth. And these all, having obtained a good report through faith, received not the promise: God having provided some better thing for us, that they without us should not be made perfect.
Hebrews 11:32-40 KJV

*My Incredible Journey* is a story of faith. Where are the people mentioned in this book now? Well, my mother is enjoying a quieter life, mentoring and influencing those around her to live a life of faith. The staff of OTAN are continuing the work to accomplish the vision from a man who was willing to do what others said was impossible. The faithful men and women in Southeast Asia who are daily doing the work of the kingdom continue to persevere in the midst of difficult circumstances and oppression … "of whom the world was not worthy!" Many have gone on to be with the Lord, but a new generation is rising up to bring the gospel to their people. Never cease praying for them.

And what a glorious reunion it is going to be one day when we are all in heaven together, rejoicing and worshiping our Lord as one big family. We will not know the lives that have been reached and touched by this ministry until that time. But what about your life now? What are you going to do next to continue on the path of your very own *Incredible Journey…*

Jana Goodwin Moritz

# About the Author

Growing up on a dairy farm in a little country village in Whitefield, Maine, Roxann Jewett Goodwin never imagined she would one day travel the world serving the Lord in areas with restricted access to Christians. With a heart to reach Chinese people for Jesus regardless of government restrictions, she and her late husband, Otis Goodwin, successfully established an unconventional mission organization to support, train, and equip national pastors to reach their own people throughout China and eventually across the Asian continent and world.

Over the last 35 years, Roxann has traveled overseas more than 50 times to eight different countries. She has met the most amazing and courageous people along the way.

She has three daughters, nine grandchildren, and several great-grandchildren. She currently lives in Fitchburg, Massachusetts, and continues to mentor and pour into women of all ages. She leads a Bible study for an amazing group of women at her church, and in her free time, she enjoys cross-stitching, baking, puzzles, and playing Words with Friends.

# How to Know for Sure that You are Going to Heaven

When asked the question, "Are you going to heaven when you die?" the vast majority of people say, "I'm not sure," or "I hope so." Wouldn't it be wonderful if you could know for sure you were going to heaven when you died? Well, you can. It is possible to have this confidence.

The Bible says:

> Whoever has the Son has life; whoever does not have God's Son does not have life. I have written this to you who believe in the name of the Son of God, so that you may have eternal life.
> 1 John 5:12-13 (NLT)

In a world full of uncertainties, the Bible says you can have the assurance of heaven at death through the Lord Jesus Christ. God has given us a plan whereby we can be saved and know it. Obedience to this plan can change you from being a "hope-so person" into a "know-so Christian."

Admit that you are a sinner and deserve hell.

> For everyone has sinned; we all fall short of God's glorious standard.
>
> Romans 3:23 (NLT)

> For the wages of sin is death (hell) …
>
> Romans 6:23a (NLT)

Believe that Jesus Christ died on the cross for your sins and rose from the grave so that you could go to heaven.

> … but the free gift of God is eternal life through Christ Jesus our Lord.
>
> Romans 6:23b (NLT)

> But God showed His great love for us by sending Christ to die for us while we were still sinners.
>
> Romans 5:8 (NLT)

> If you openly declare that Jesus is Lord and believe in your heart that God raised him from the dead, you will be saved.
>
> Romans 10:9 (NLT)

Call upon the Lord through prayer for salvation.

> For everyone who calls on the name of the Lord will be saved.
>
> Romans 10:13 (NLT)

> Indeed, the "right time" is now. Today is the day of salvation.
>
> 2 Corinthians 6:2b (NLT)

> But to all who believed him and accepted him, he gave the right to become children of God.
>
> John 1:12 (NLT)

If you would like to receive Jesus Christ as your personal Lord and Savior, talk with God through the following prayer:

> *Dear God,*
>
> *I am a sinner. Because of my sin, I deserve to spend eternity in hell. I believe that Jesus died on the cross, was buried, and rose from the grave for my sins. I, therefore, turn from my sins and put my faith in Jesus Christ to get me to heaven. Thank you for saving me today and help me to serve you the rest of my life. In Jesus' name, Amen.*

You became a Christian the moment you received Christ. Don't trust your feelings for they will change. Take God at His word and believe His promises. You can now say, "I have received Christ, and on the authority of God's word, I am going to heaven when I die."

## What to do Next

> Rather, you must grow in the grace and knowledge of our Lord and Savior Jesus Christ.
>
> 2 Peter 3:18a (NLT)